ANGLO CONCERTINA
FROM BEGINNER TO MASTER

Cohen Braithwaite-Kilcoyne

Rollston Press

Anglo Concertina from Beginner to Master
by Cohen Braithwaite-Kilcoyne

All rights reserved. No part of this book may be reproduced, scanned, transmitted or distributed in any printed or electronic form without the prior permission of the author except in the case of brief quotations embodied in articles or reviews.

Copyright © 2022 Cohen Braithwaite-Kilcoyne

ISBN-13: 978-1-953208-04-0

All titles are in the public domain unless otherwise noted.

Front cover artwork by Rosie Hood

ROLLSTON PRESS
1717 Ala Wai Blvd #1703
Honolulu, HI 96815
USA

info@rollstonpress.com

Preface

I first learned of Cohen Braithwaite-Kilcoyne through a University of Leeds recital video that concertina player Adrian Brown brought to the attention of the greater concertina community.

It was filmed in a concert hall in front of a live audience and featured a very young and very talented young man playing the 2-row melodeon and the Anglo concertina, mostly playing solo but occasionally accompanied by an organ or a piano.

The recital lasted thirty-eight minutes and showcased a variety of folk tunes and intricate classical pieces played with an astonishing vigor and musicality, and with a confidence usually only found in players of much greater age.

From quiet passages of great subtlety to strenuous doppler effects, the video clearly showed a player of great skill in full command, who completely mastered what his instruments were capable of.

You can see the video here:

UNIVERSITY OF LEEDS SCHOOL OF MUSIC – FINAL RECITAL 2017

https://livestream.com/uol/final-recitals-17/videos/157705262

Realizing that someone with this much ability and training would have a lot to offer to players of the Anglo concertina, I reached out to Cohen, and he graciously offered to share his insights and instruction through this tutor. He has been an absolute delight to work with and brings a methodical dedication to teaching and learning that shows in every page of this book.

Every tune is accompanied by a smartphone-scannable QR code that links to a video of Cohen playing the tune exactly as it appears in the book. He plays a large 45-button Anglo, but each tune is arranged specifically for the 30-button Anglo concertina with Wheatstone/Lachenal accidentals.

Although I have been playing the concertina for many many years, I have personally learned so much more from Cohen's approach and teaching. I hope you too will find it to be a wealth of tunes and techniques that will advance your playing and help you enjoy your playing all the more.

Gary Coover
Editor / Publisher
Rollston Press

TABLE OF CONTENTS

Introduction 7
Keyboard and Tablature 8

Chapter 1: Playing in the Home Keys 12
1.1 Waltz 13
1.2 Such a Wife as Willy Had 14
1.3 Bryan O'Lynn 14
1.4 The Christmas Tale 15
1.5 The Magic Girdle 16
1.6 The Devil in a Bush 18
1.7 West Cottage Hornpipe 19
1.8 Rattling Morgan 21
1.9 The Tempest 22
1.10 All Around the Maypole See How They Trot 23
1.11 Marybone Assembly 25
1.12 Fishes in the Sea 30
1.13 Favourite Banjo Breakdown 31
1.14 Sailor's Hornpipe 32
1.15 Cat's Polka 33
1.16 Beautiful Star 34

Chapter 2: Beginning with Chordal Accompaniment 36
2.1 Minasi Number 3 37
2.2 Minasi Number 7 40
2.3 Waltz 41
2.4 Tyroler Waltzer 42
2.5 Westwood Park 44
2.6 Lichfield Races 45
2.7 Lady Cathcart 46
2.8 The Exile 47
2.9 The Birmingham March 49
2.10 The Labarynth 50
2.11 Tekeli 51
2.12 Honey Moon 52

2.13 Paddy Wack 53
2.14 Frogmore Farm 54
2.15 Miss Gayton's Hornpipe 55

Chapter 3: New Keys 57
3.1 Ellingham Assembly 58
3.2 Now or Never 59
3.3 King's Polka 60
3.4 The Philosopher's Jigg 61
3.5 Trip to London 62
3.6 Saxon Hornpipe 64
3.7 Take a Dance 69
3.8 The Unfortunate Cup of Tea 70
3.9 Wilkes's Wriggle 71
3.10 The Fiddler's Jig 73
3.11 Welsh Fusiliers 75
3.12 Cure For All Grief 76
3.13 Harliquin Air 77
3.14 Two and Two 78

Chapter 4: Chordal Accompaniment 80
4.1 Union Waltz 83
4.2 Buds of May 84
4.3 Spring's Waltz 85
4.4 Freedom and Liberty 86
4.5 Rakish Highlandman 87

Chapter 5: Playing in Octaves 88
5.1 Chamberlain Election 89
5.2 Nineteenth of May 91
5.3 The London Camp 93
5.4 Marey's Dream 94

Chapter 6: Alternate Approaches to Accompaniment 96
6.1a Cotillon 96
6.1b Cotillon 97
6.2 French March 98

6.3 Prince William 100

6.4 When once I lay with another Man's Wife 101

6.5 Holborn March 102

6.6 Grano's March 104

6.7 Windsor Terrace 105

6.8 Maid in the Wood 106

Chapter 7: Hymns 108

7.1 Dover 108

7.2 Colchester 109

7.3 The Vesper's Hymn 110

7.4 Bridgeford 111

7.5 Cambridge New 112

7.6 Cambridge Short Tune 113

7.7 Oxford Tune 114

7.8 The Martyr's Tune 115

Chapter 8: Baroque 116

8.1 Telemann's 5th Fantasia for solo flute 117

8.2 Westhoff's 4th Partita for solo violin 125

Sources 135

Video Links 138

Bio 141

Tune Index 143

Introduction

This book is the culmination of over a decade of fascination and infatuation with the Anglo concertina. Throughout my career as an Anglo concertina player, I have increasingly been interested in exploring repertoire that is considered 'outside of the norm' for Anglo players and in exploring the ways in which the Anglo concertina was played during its heyday in the nineteenth and early twentieth centuries. In some circles today, the Anglo is seen as the poor relation to English or Duet concertinas, only suitable for English morris tunes or Irish reels. If we look at the multitude of sources relating to Anglo concertina playing in the 19th or early 20th centuries, we can see that this is not the case; the Anglo was used for a huge range of styles, some very complex.

One of the clearest areas in which the Anglo is often 'written off' is the idea that it can only play in a couple of keys. This attitude has often led players to not venture outside of the home keys of their instruments. In fact, a thirty key Anglo concertina is chromatic over the range of nearly three octaves and exploring some of these lesser used keys can be thrilling and open a range of new repertoires and sonic areas. I firmly believe that players in the 19th century must have used the Anglo in far more than its two home keys; surely the instruments would not have evolved to have thirty or more keys if there were no need to play outside of the home keys. Additionally, many historical tutor books focus extensively on playing in broad range of keys, some even giving scales and/or chords for every key.

Nevertheless, I have tried to balance this interest in the historical styles of playing with the needs of 21st century Anglo concertina players. For instance, although playing in a wide number of keys was much more common in the 19th century, I have generally kept keys restrained to those most used today- after all there is little call for concertinas to play in A flat in most modern circumstances!

This book is not a detailed analysis into the ways in which the Anglo concertina was played in the 19th and early 20th centuries rather it is intended as a player's guide for the concertina, drawing influence from early concertina styles. Some of the material in this book has been taken directly from early concertina tutors, while other material has been drawn from 18th and 19th century tune books and manuscripts- a full list of sources is available at the end of this book.

The book is divided into chapters with each chapter being based around a different theme or style of concertina playing. Each of these chapters gets gradually more complex as it progresses and each chapter, overall, is more complex than the one that proceeds it. To help you navigate this, each tune has been assigned an ability level from one to seven- taking you through from beginner to master.

Keyboard and Tablature

Here is the button numbering system for 30-button Anglo concertinas in the key of C/G:

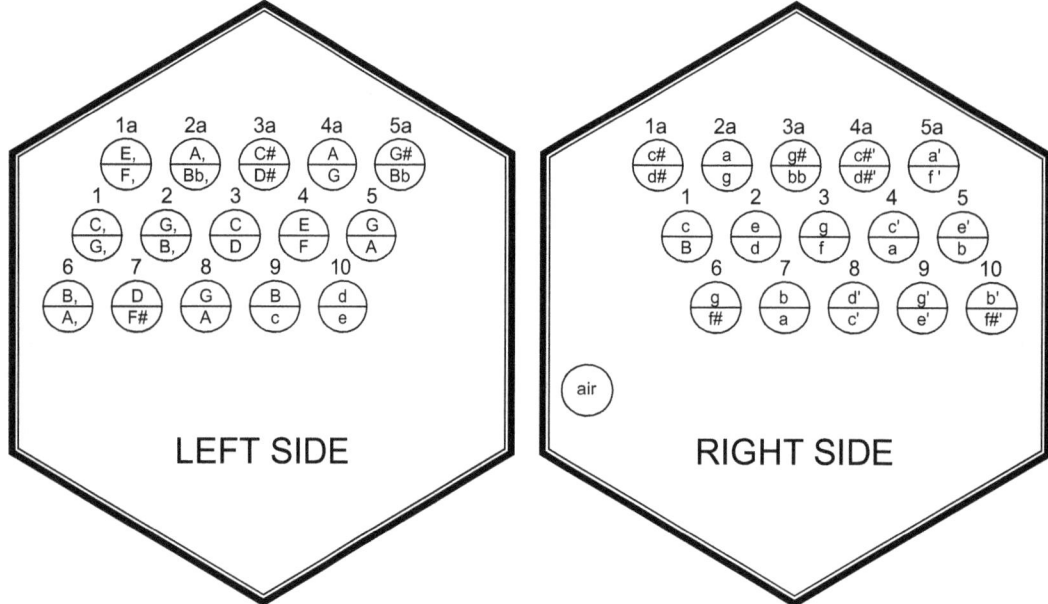

Low notes are on the left side of the instrument and high notes are on the right. Notes shown above the line are on the push, notes shown below the line are on the pull. Standard abc notation has been used to show the pitches of the notes.

How the tablature works in this book:

- The buttons are numbered using the "1a-10" numbering system for each side.
- Buttons on the right-hand side are shown above the musical notes.
- Buttons on the left-hand side are shown below the musical notes.
- Notes on the push are shown by button number only.
- Notes on the pull are shown by button number with a line across the top.
- Long phrases all on the pull will have one long continuous line above the button numbers.
- Notes that are held longer indicated with dashed lines after the button number.

Button Maps

Each tune also has a Button Map showing the buttons needed to play that particular tune:

Buttons played

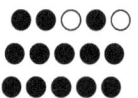 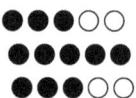

Fingering

Since everyone's hands are different, I have given almost no indications for which fingers to use in this book. There are however a few general rules in relation to finger usage that I would recommend keeping in mind for concertina playing:

- Try to avoid crossing (using the same finger for two consecutive notes on two different buttons).
- Find a comfortable 'home position' for tunes- a hand position in which the majority of the tune can be played and think carefully about where and how you might deviate from this position.
- Use all four fingers on both hands.

Air button

The use of the air button on the Anglo concertina can be something of a fine art, but it is essential that you are comfortable with it. Many tunes are imbalanced in their bellows directions, which can leave the player struggling for bellows capacity, however, creative usage of the air button can alleviate this.

Air button usage is not indicated in this book, since it is virtually impossible to notate a 'one-size-fits-all' approach. I would recommend spending a little time getting used to the feeling of tapping your air button in tunes to get a quick rush of air.

One challenge of air button usage is making sure that your tone remains even while using the button- there is a temptation to push or pull much harder on the bellows when using the air button to grab more air, however this is best avoided since it can create a sudden surge in the dynamic level. Experiment to find what works best for your concertina and for you as a player.

Difficulty Levels

Level 1: Single note tunes on a single row

Level 2: Single note tunes with some row crossing, some basic harmonic style tunes

Level 3: More complex row crossing, also some simple harmonic style tunes with 2-3 chords

Level 4: More complex harmonic style tunes in home keys and D

Level 5: More complex harmonic style tunes- particularly those keys other than C, G and D

Level 6: Tunes with independent voicing or in complex keys

Level 7: Advanced tunes

Some tips for practice

1) Break it down:

The best way to tackle just about anything in music is to break it down into small manageable chunks- maybe just a couple of bars. Practice these chunks individually until you are comfortable with them and then gradually join them together into the full tune. Now try playing the whole tune through, if there are any bits that you find yourself constantly tripping over, take those out of the tune and practice them until you are more comfortable with them, then try joining them back into the tune.

2) Use a metronome

Use a metronome in practice, starting at a slow tempo and gradually building it up.

3) Sing

Try singing or humming a tune while you are in the process of learning it. This will help you to get the melody into your head without you needing to think about the technical side of playing it. Once the tune is ingrained in your head, it will then be easier for your fingers to find their way.

4) Play from memory

Playing from memory can be one of the best ways to ensure that your playing becomes more fluid and musical. The less time you spend reading music or tablature, the more time you can focus on making your playing musically pleasing.

5) Practice is key

Try to practice regularly and efficiently. Little and often is better than an occasional long practice session; it is better to practice for fifteen minutes every day than to do a two-hour session once a week.

6) Listen

Listen to as many concertina players as you can, try to analyse their techniques and take elements that you like to incorporate into your own style. Most importantly, listen to yourself; try to constantly evaluate your playing, one of the best things you can do is record yourself playing and listen back with a critical ear, trying to take notice of what sounds good and what needs to be improved.

7) Be realistic

Be realistic in you aims. It is always good to stretch yourself as a musician but going too far beyond your ability level can be counterproductive. Some of the material in this book is quite complex- recognise when material is beyond your capabilities and if that is, revisit it after working on something easier.

Method for practicing problem areas:

1) Identify the problem area.

2) Take that bit out of the tune.

3) Play through it slowly a few times, try to identify what it is that you are tripping up on- sometimes at this point a small adjustment in something such as fingering may fix the issue.

4) Repeat the phrase starting slowly, once you can play it slowly, get a little faster.

5) Once you can play it 5-10 times in a row without stumbling, try putting it back in the tune. If joining it back into the music creates issues, try joining one note at a time as in the example below:

If for example you were having problems with the second line of The Christmas Tale (tune 1.4):

By going over it a few times, you have identified that it is the third and fourth bar that you are tripping up on- take those bars out of the tune and then try playing through them as outlined above.

Once you can play those comfortably, introduce one note from the previous bar as follows.

Once you can do that, introduce a couple more notes from the previous bar.

Continue this process for all the notes immediately before and after the problem phrase until it fits back into the tune.

Chapter 1: Playing in the Home Keys

Through this chapter, we will begin exploring the Anglo concertina in its simplest form- playing single note tunes in the home keys (C and G).

The 'single note' style in its basic form is the simplest way to play the concertina, however, in experienced hands, this approach can yield spectacular results. The single note style features in many early concertina tutors and is used in almost all concertina playing traditions. We will begin this chapter by looking at playing in the two home keys, first on the row, then with row crossing. Finally, we will look at embellishing single note tunes with ornamentation and punctuating chords.

The key of C

On a 30 key C/G Anglo concertina, they key of C is played using the notes of the middle row. Exercises 1.1 and 1.2 show the fingering for a C major scale using just the notes available on the middle row.

Exercise 1.1

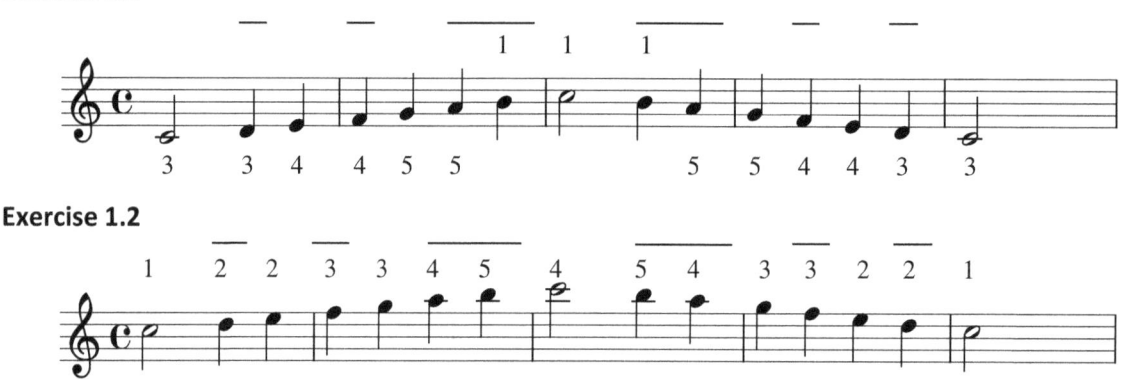

Exercise 1.2

Exercises 1.1 and 1.2 are the first of many scales that will feature in this book. There are several ways to play scales, and I would recommend practicing all of these to develop your playing, these include:

- Staccato: short notes, snappy.
- Legato: smooth.
- Varying dynamics: try loud (forte) or quiet (piano) or try playing alternate notes in different dynamics or try gradually getting louder (crescendo) or quieter (diminuendo).
- Saying the name of each note as you play it.

To get your fingers round the C row, try exercise 1.3, a broken chord exercise:

Exercise 1.3

Now that you have got your fingers moving round the C row, here are a selection of reasonably simple tunes using just the notes available on the C row.

Tune 1.1

Waltz

Difficulty Level 1

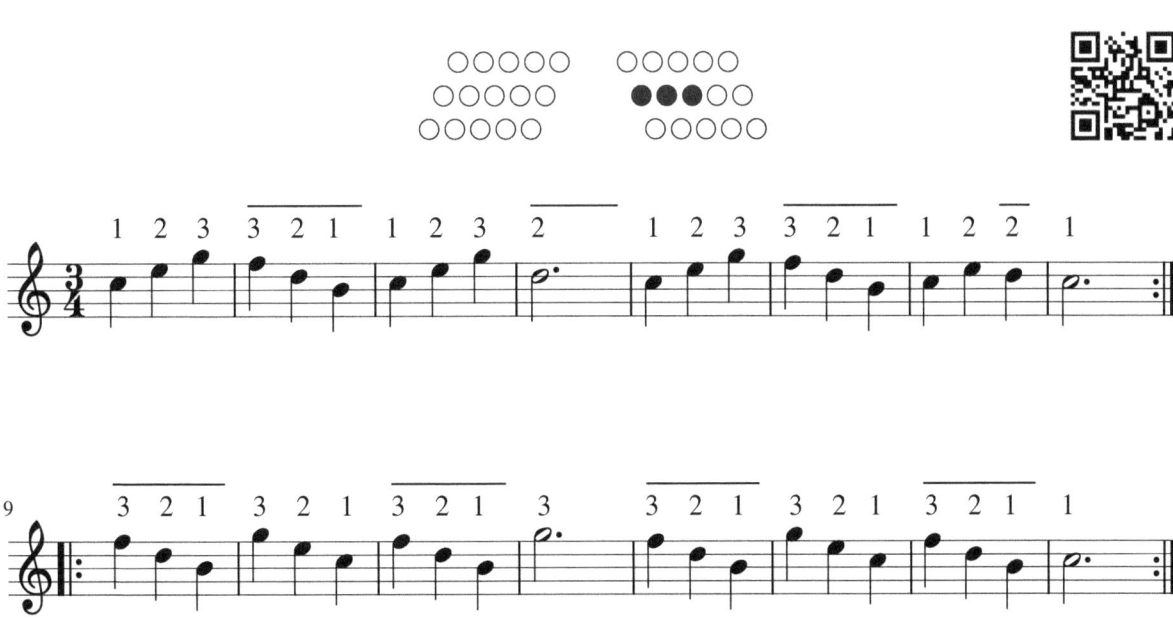

Anglo Concertina from Beginner to Master

Tune 1.2

Such a Wife as Willy Had

Difficulty Level 1

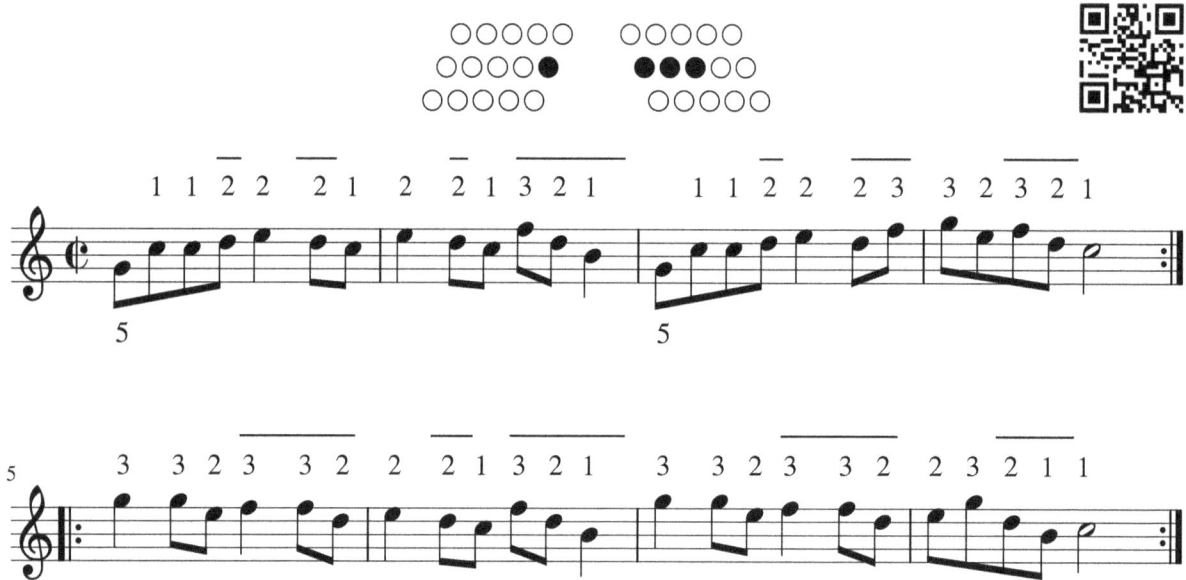

Tune 1.3

Bryan O'Lynn

Difficulty Level 1

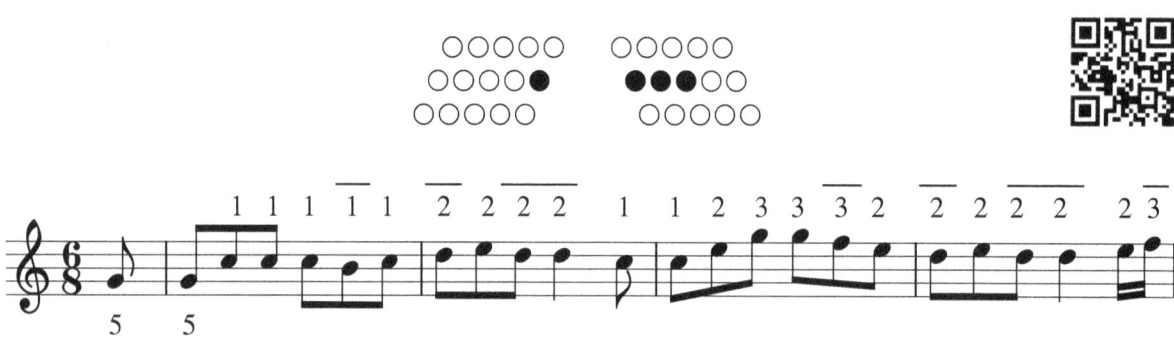

Tune 1.4

The Christmas Tale

Difficulty Level 1

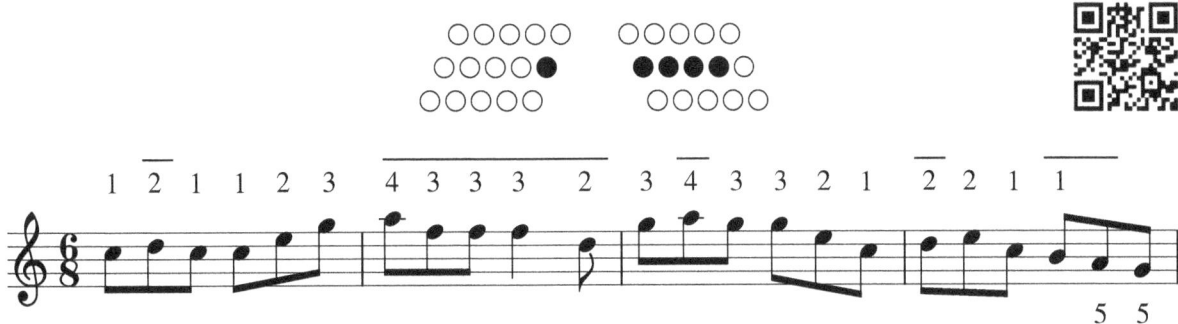

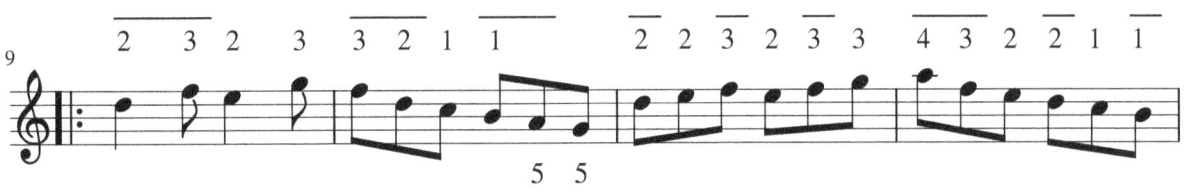

Tune 1.5

The Magic Girdle

Difficulty Level 1

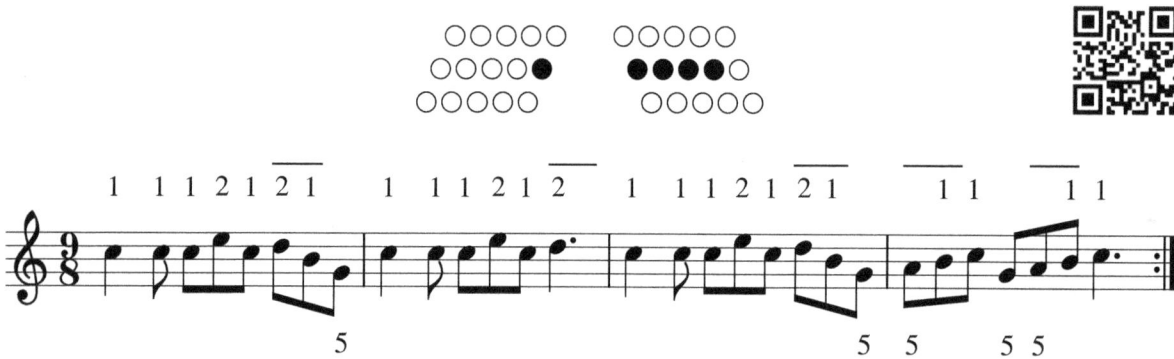

The key of G

The key of G is the second home key for a C/G Anglo concertina. Exercises 1.4 and 1.5 are basic G major scales, you will notice that the fingering for these are identical to the C major scales above, just moved onto the G row.

Exercise 1.4

Exercise 1.5

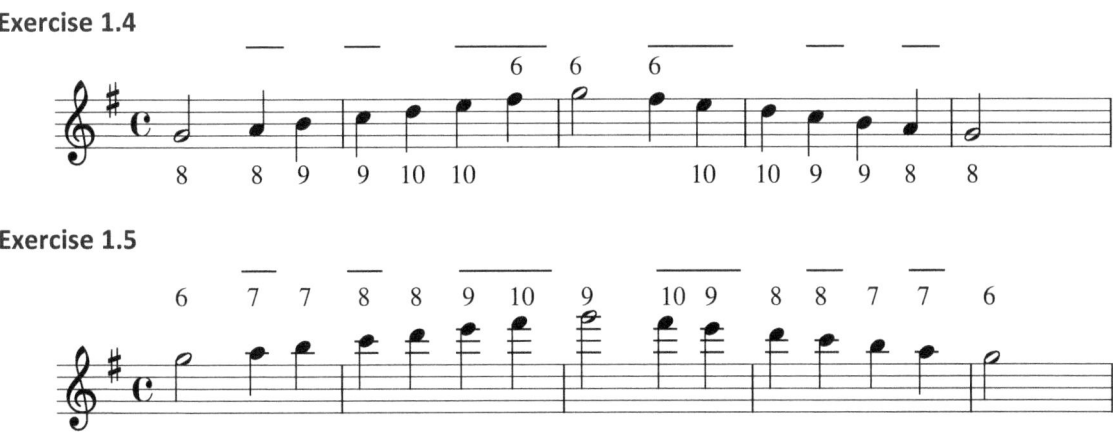

Here is a selection of tunes in G that use the notes on the G row.

Tune 1.6

The Devil in a Bush

Difficulty Level 1

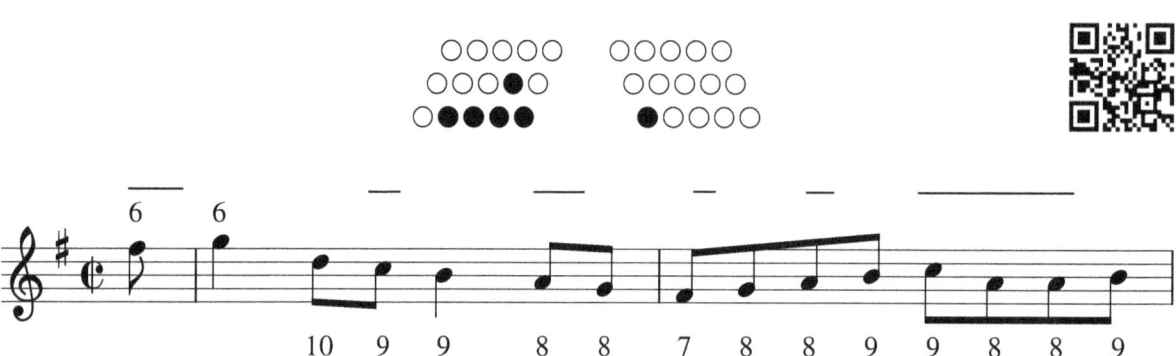

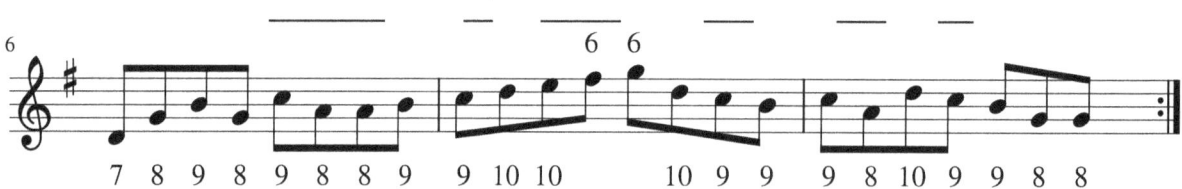

Tune 1.7

West Cottage Hornpipe

Difficulty Level 1

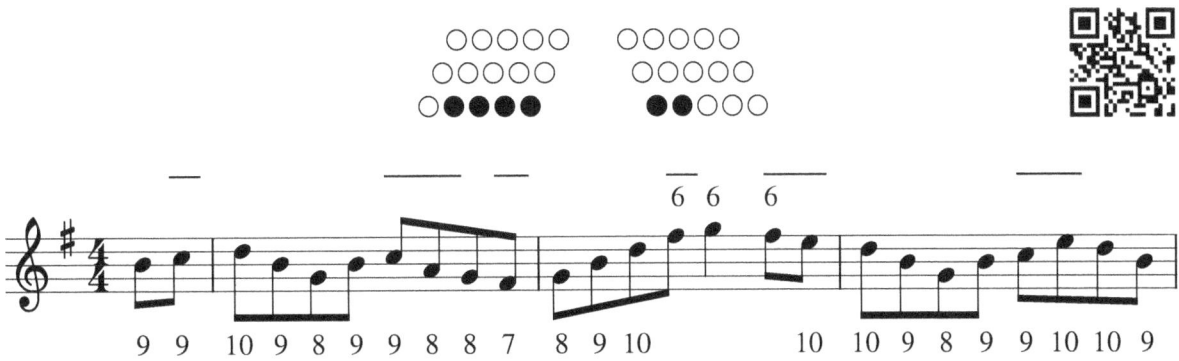

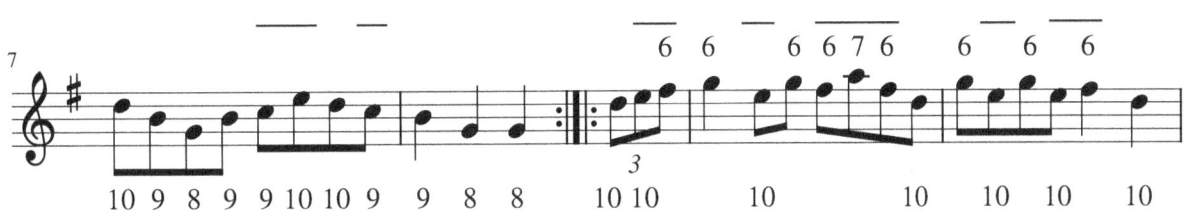

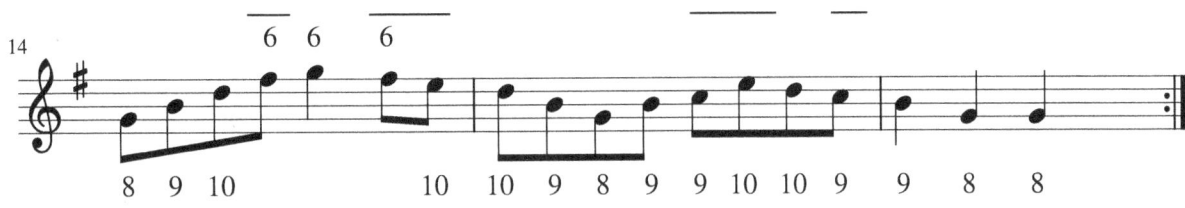

Row crossing in G

The technique of 'row crossing' is often useful for playing in the key of G. Row crossing involves using notes from across all three rows and from both sides of the instrument in playing and can reduce the need for constant bellows direction changes thus creating a smoother articulation and opening up further possibilities in the area of chordal accompaniment.

Here is a G scale over two octaves, using row crossing, making use of almost all available positions for the notes of a G scale in the two bottom octaves.

Exercise 1.6

Now try the following broken chord exercise in G. You will notice that part 1 of the following exercise is almost identical to exercise 1.3 but moved onto the G row. Part 2 uses the lower octave and crosses over to the C and accidental rows.

Exercise 1.7

Now try the following selection of tunes in G that use row crossing.

Tune 1.8

Rattling Morgan

Difficulty Level 2

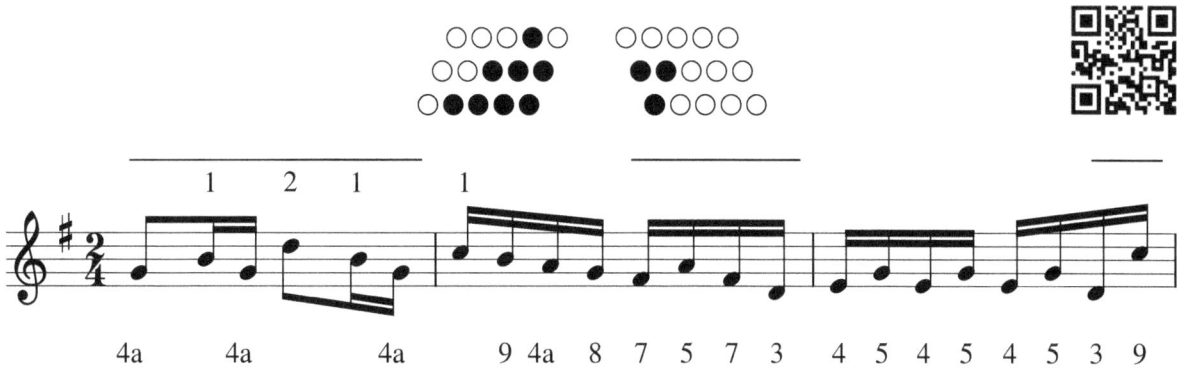

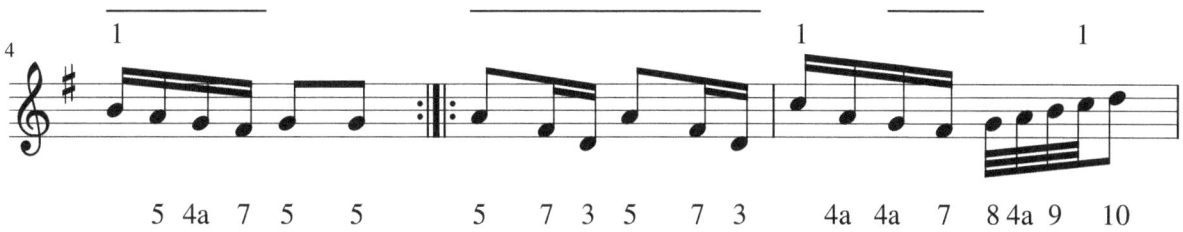

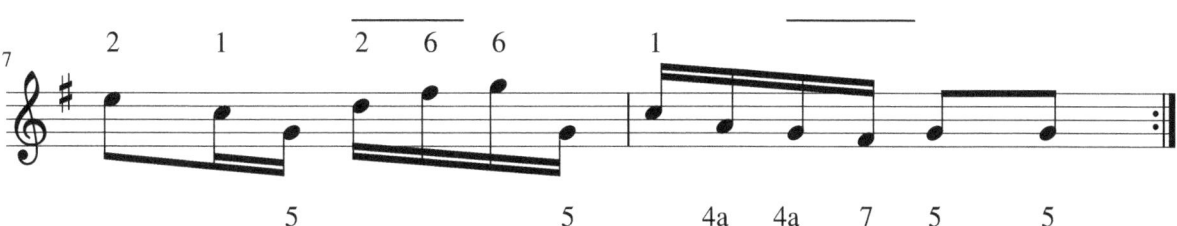

Tune 1.9

The Tempest

Difficulty Level 2

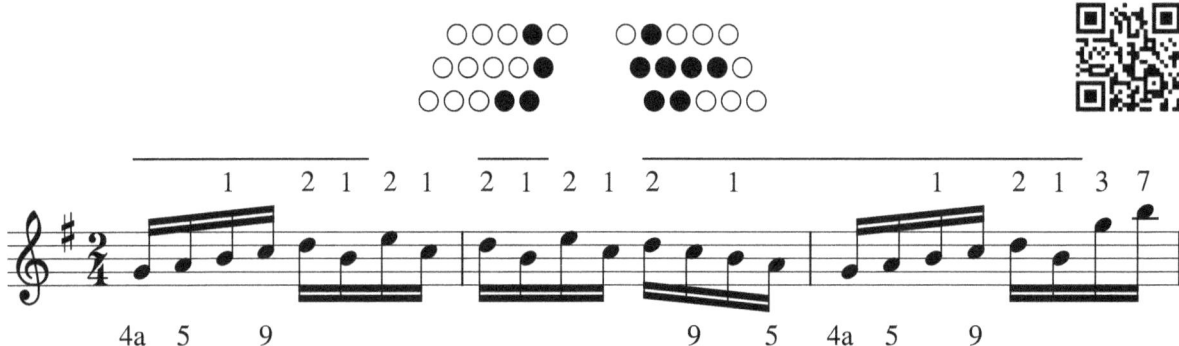

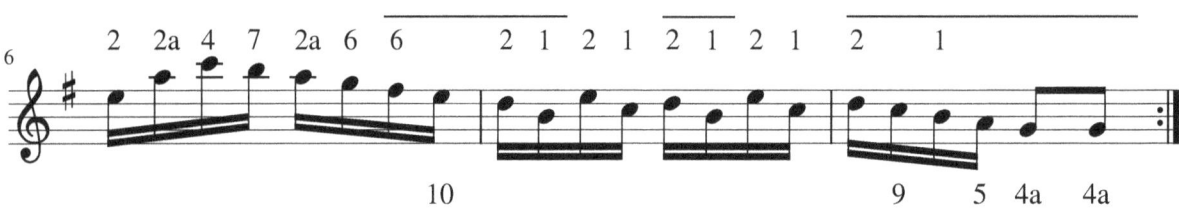

Tune 1.10

All Around the Maypole See How They Trot

Difficulty Level 2

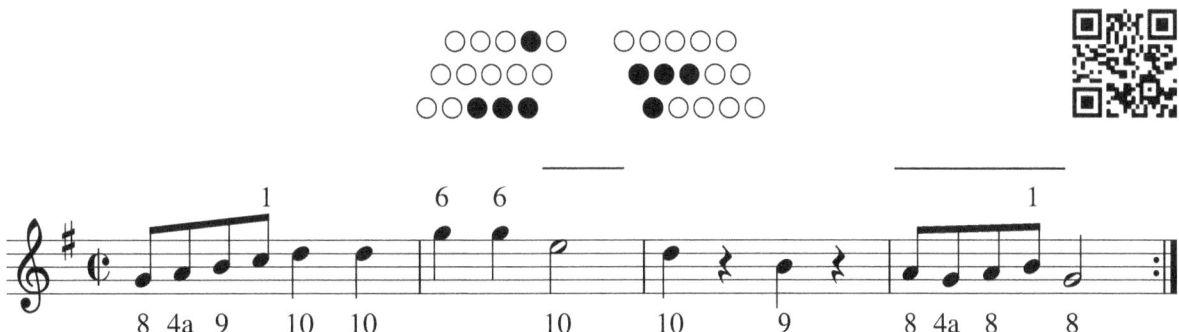

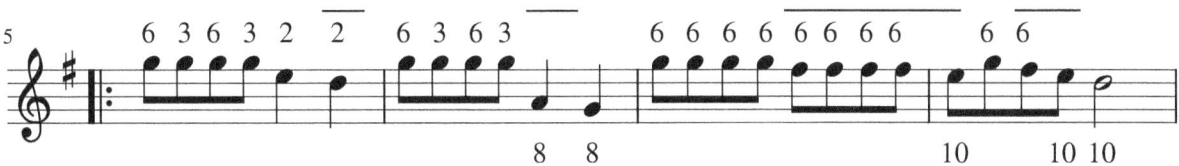

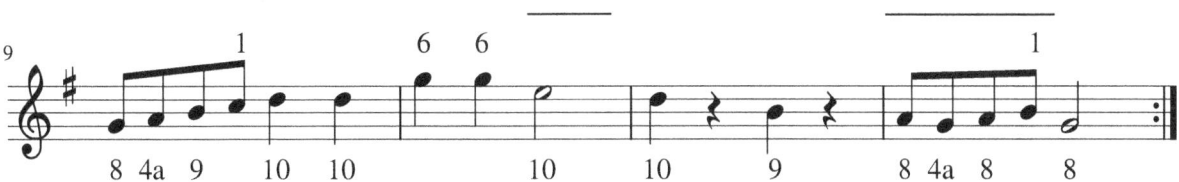

Note the rests in bars 3 and 11 of 'All Around the Maypole See How They Trot', try to keep these as crisp and clear as possibly.

Also notice the repeated notes in bars 5, 6 and 7- you will see that through the tab, two different approached are used to play these, exercises 1.8 and 1.9 below go into more detail regarding this.

Repeated note technique one: two buttons

The first of the two techniques for repeated notes appears in bars 5 and 6. In this case you alternate between two buttons that produce the same note- on a standard 30 key Anglo concertina, there are four places on the keyboard that this can be achieved without changing directions on the bellows, they are as follows:

   Left hand buttons 5 and 8, push both play a G

   Left hand buttons 5 and 8, pull both play an A

   Right hand buttons 3 and 6 push both play a G

   Right hand buttons 4 and 7 pull both play an A

Alternating between buttons in these four positions can be an effective way to achieve repeated notes as shown in exercise 1.8 below:

Exercise 1.8

Repeated note technique two: double fingering

The second technique for repeated notes is to use double fingering- this is used in bar 7 of the tune above. In this technique two separate fingers alternate to press the same button as shown in the illustration below:

Once you can do this on one button comfortably, try it using a different combination of fingers (the above example uses 1 and 2; try with 2 and 3 or 3 and 4) and try it across the keyboard. Exercise 1.9 is an ascending G major scale with repeated notes- try double fingering this:

Exercise 1.9

Tune 1.11

Marybone Assembly

Difficulty Level 3

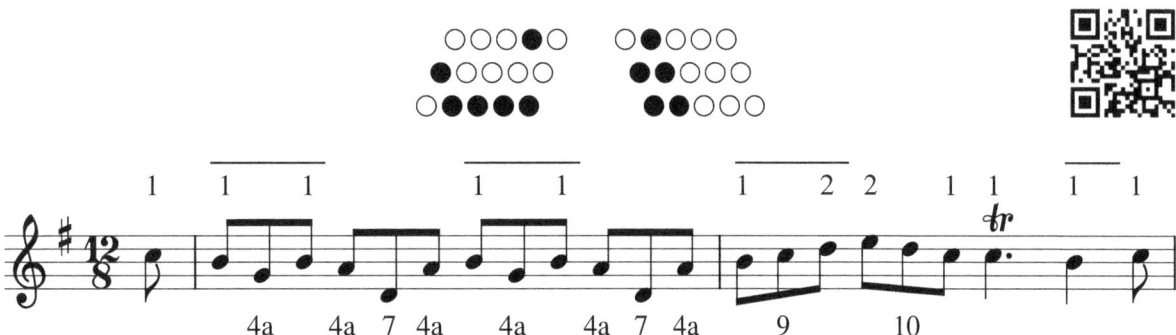

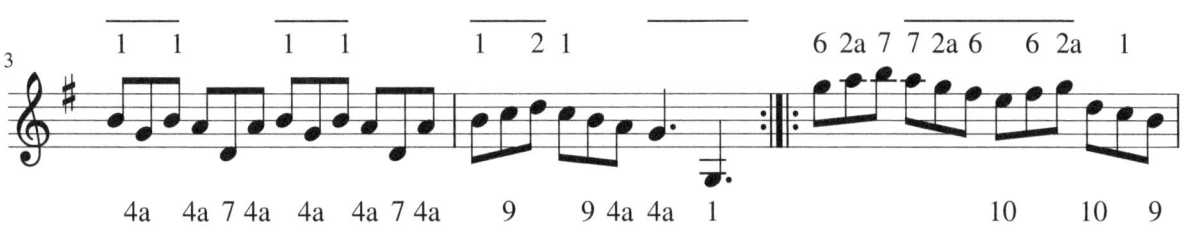

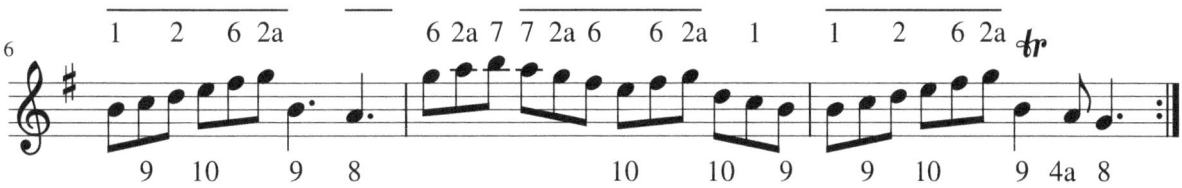

Ornaments

Trill

You will notice that there are trills (marked tr) in bars 2 and 8 of Marybone Assembly. The trill is achieved by alternating between the written melody note and the note above it. In the cases of the trills for the notes above these would be as follows:

The trill is just one example of a musical ornament that can be used in your playing to embellish your melodies. At this point, we will briefly explore some other basic ornaments and show how these can be used in 'Such a Wife as Willy Had' (tune 1.2).

Grace notes

Grace notes are a very common form of ornamentation. Broadly speaking, a grace note is a note either above or below the written melody note that is played quickly before the melody note. Grace notes come in two forms- the appoggiatura (shown on the left of the example below) which is a longer grace note taking roughly half the length of the written note and the acciaccatura or crush note (shown on the right of the example below) which is played much quicker before the start of the main note. Acciaccaturas are used more commonly in folk music.

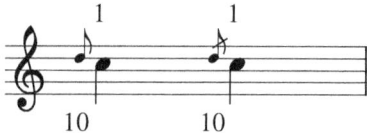

The example below shows two possible ways of embellishing bar 5 of 'Such a Wife as Willy Had' using acciaccaturas. The first example shows how acciaccaturas can be used either a scale degree above or below the melody note for decoration, while the second example uses a chromatic grace note (i.e. one outside of the diatonic C major scale used in the tune).

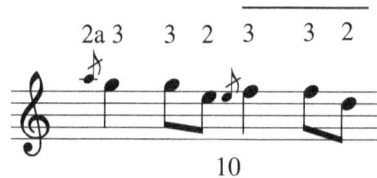

The above example shows just two possibilities for grace notes that could be used in this bar, experiment some of the other options to see what you can come up with, some grace notes work better than others. As a broad rule, grace notes are more convincing when they are either a musical semitone or tone above or below the written melody note.

Zip

The zip is a concertina specific ornament that is a development of the grace note, essentially being a series of grace notes played before the melody note. Zips usually use the notes of an arpeggio- it is for this reason that they are particularly effective on the Anglo concertina since these notes can be easily played by running through the notes on a row. Zips appear in two forms, an upward zip where the melody note is preceded by a zip that comes from below and rises, or a downward zip where the melody note is preceded by a zip that comes from above and descends. In the example below I have shown how bar one of 'Such a Wife as Willy Had' can be decorated with a downward zip and how bar five can be decorated with an upward zip.

Mordant

Mordants come in two forms, upper mordants and lower mordants. Mordants are achieve by interrupting the main melody note with either a note from above (upper mordant) or below (lower mordant) before returning to the written melody note, as shown in the example below.

The example below shows how the opening bars of 'Such a Wife as Willy Had' can be decorated with both upper and lower mordants (along with a grace note). The example first shows how this would appear in written music, and then shows how this would be played.

Anglo Concertina from Beginner to Master

Turn

A final ornament for this chapter is the turn. This ornament is achieved by first playing the main melody note, followed by the note above, then back to the main note, then one down before finishing on the main note. This is expressed in the example below.

The following example shows how a turn could be incorporated into bar 5 of 'Such a Wife as Willy Had' again first shown as it would appear in music, then shown as it would be played.

To conclude this section on ornamentation, I have written out 'Such a Wife as Willy Had' featuring example ornamentation. The top stave in this shown how these ornaments would be written, while the lower stave shows how these would be played.

Adding chords for punctuation and decoration

In the following chapters we will explore in detail how chords can be used for accompaniment, however, another effective way to use chords is to use them for punctuation and embellishment, almost as another form of ornamentation. This style of playing appears in a number of historic tutors and is an effective way to add interest to single note tunes. Four of the following five tunes come directly from historic tutors; only tune 1.15 comes from a non-concertina-based source, though it is set very much in the same style.

Tune 1.12

Fishes in the Sea

Difficulty Level 2

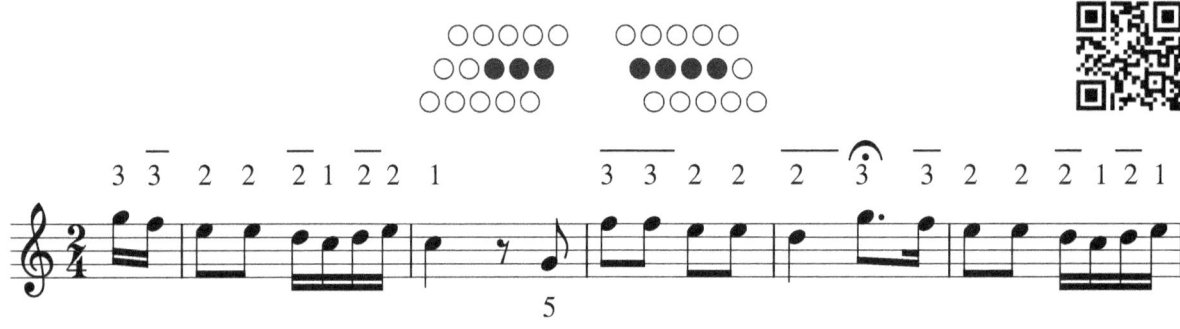

Tune 1.13

Favourite Banjo Breakdown

Difficulty Level 3

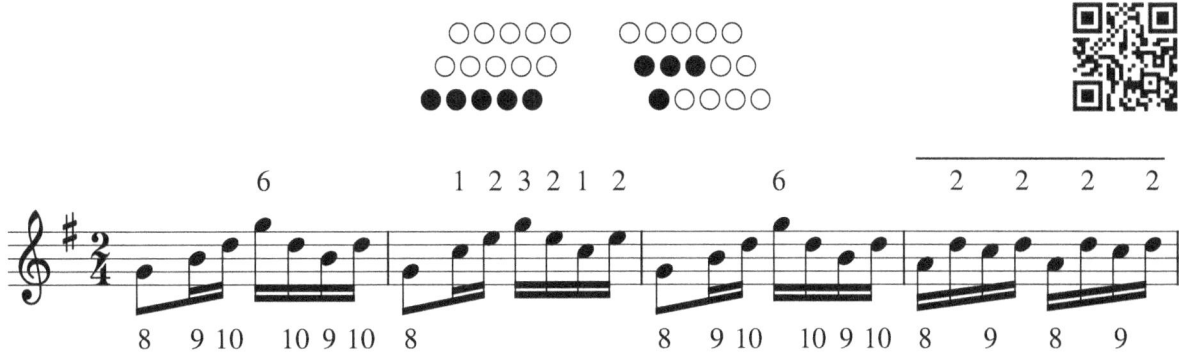

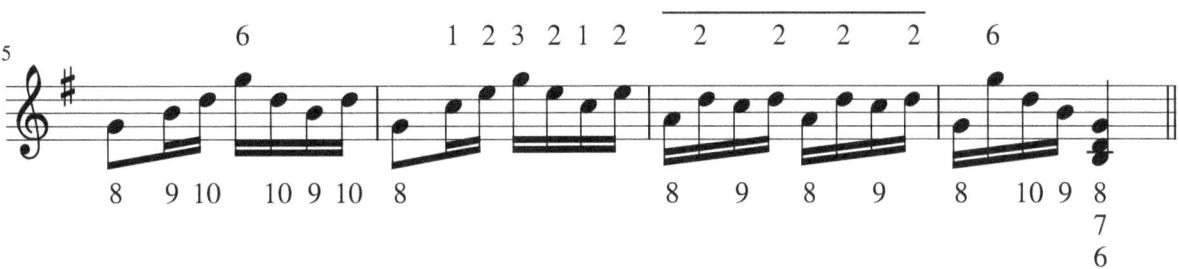

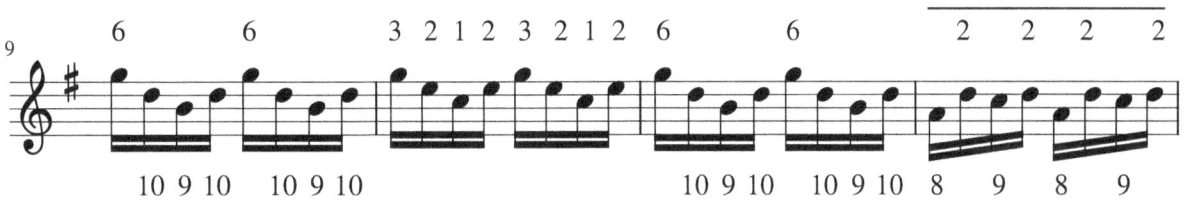

Tune 1.14

Sailor's Hornpipe

Difficulty Level 3

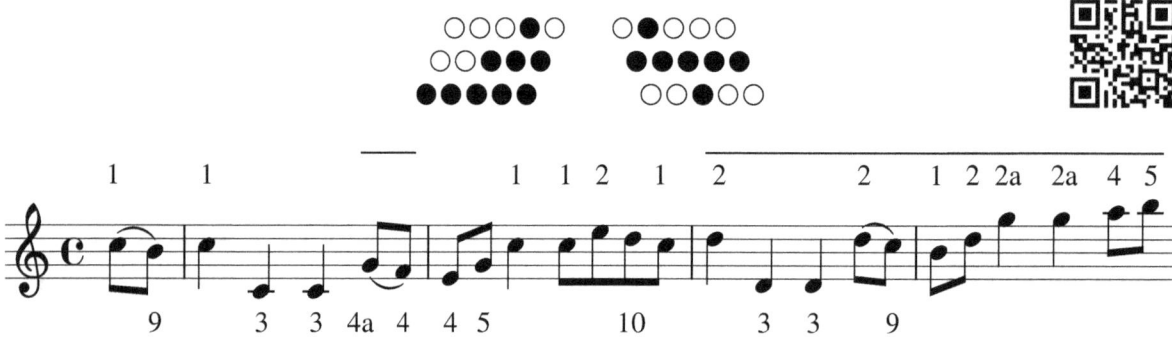

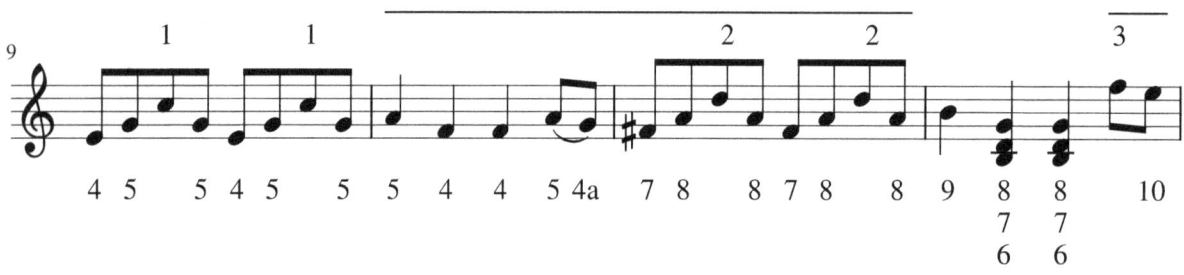

Tune 1.15

The Cat's Polka

Difficulty Level 3

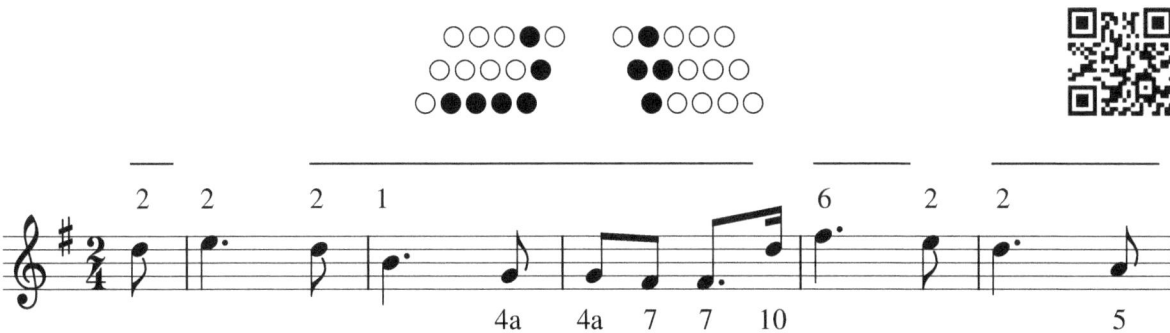

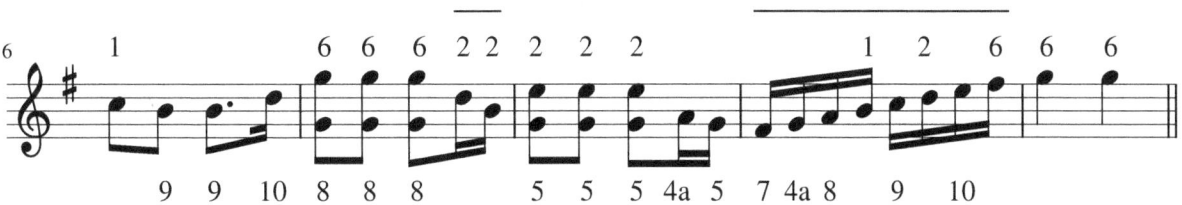

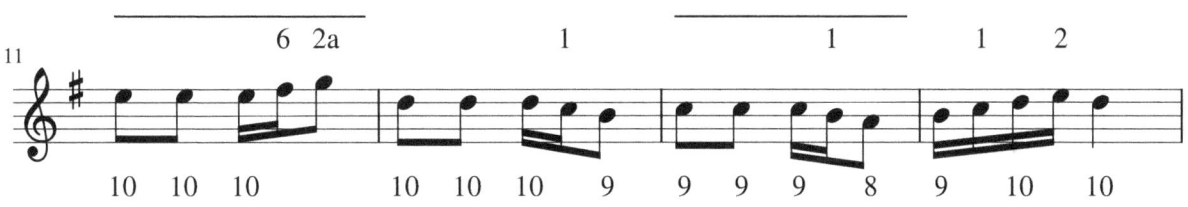

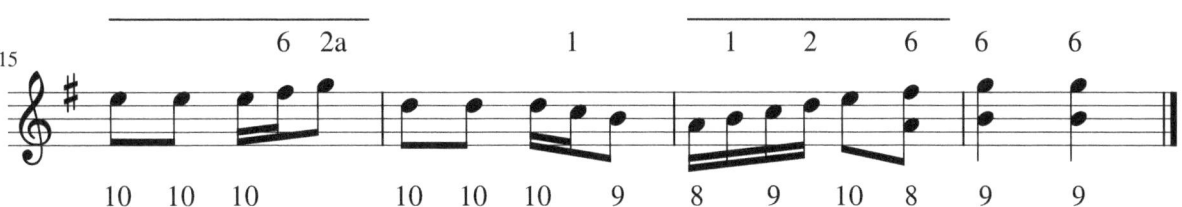

Tune 1.16

Beautiful Star

Difficulty Level 3

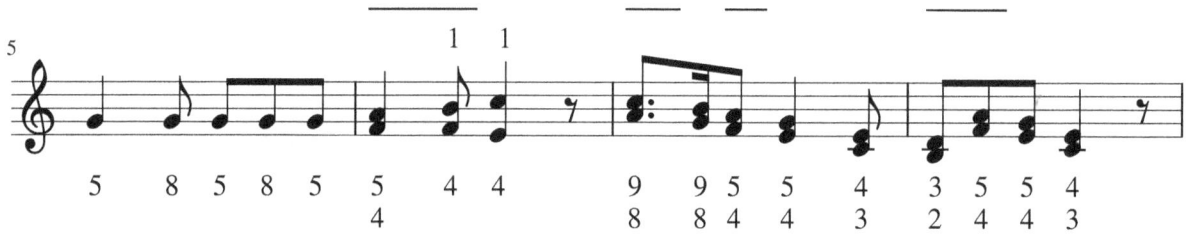

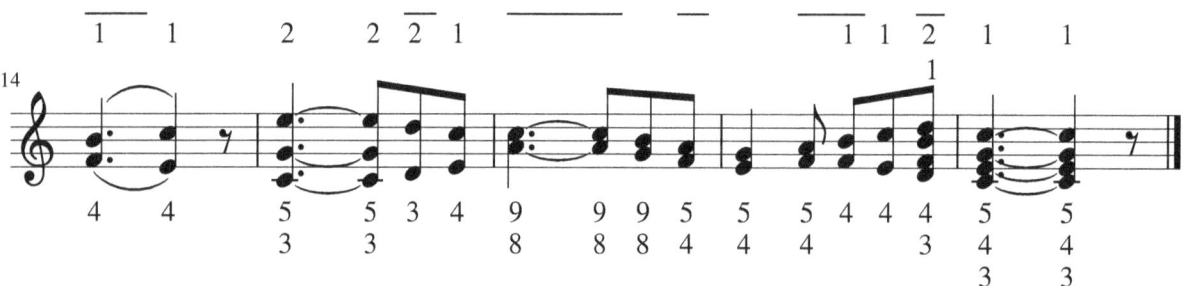

Concluding remarks

Through this first chapter, you should now be comfortably with playing tunes in the two home keys of C and G, both in an 'on the row' style and a 'cross-row' style. You should also have some idea of how to perform some key ornaments and how to add chords for decoration and emphasis. These skills will form an essential groundwork for the rest of this book and for Anglo concertina playing in general.

To build on the skills of this chapter, I would recommend going back through the tunes at the beginning of the chapter and experiment with adding ornamentation where possible. Try also adding decorative chords, focusing first on adding chords to the end of sections. Generally, you will want to use the chord of the key signature in these places (i.e. a C chord for tunes in C, a G chord for tunes in G, etc.), if you are unsure about chord shapes, we will explore those in greater depth in the following chapters.

Chapter 2: Beginning with Chordal Accompaniment

Having explored how to play single note tunes in the home keys of C and G in the previous chapter, we will now begin to look at how chordal accompaniment can be added to tunes in these keys. One of the most appealing parts of the Anglo concertina is its ability for you to become a 'one-man-band' playing tunes and accompaniments simultaneously and for this reason, chordal style playing features prominently in historic tutors and in almost all traditional styles of concertina playing.

Tunes in C

Playing in C gives the most scope for rich chords and it is the key in which chordal playing is generally the most intuitive. The first four tunes in this chapter all come from historic concertina tutors, providing a glimpse into the 19th century style of chordal playing.

Tune 2.1

Minasi Number 3

Difficulty Level 2

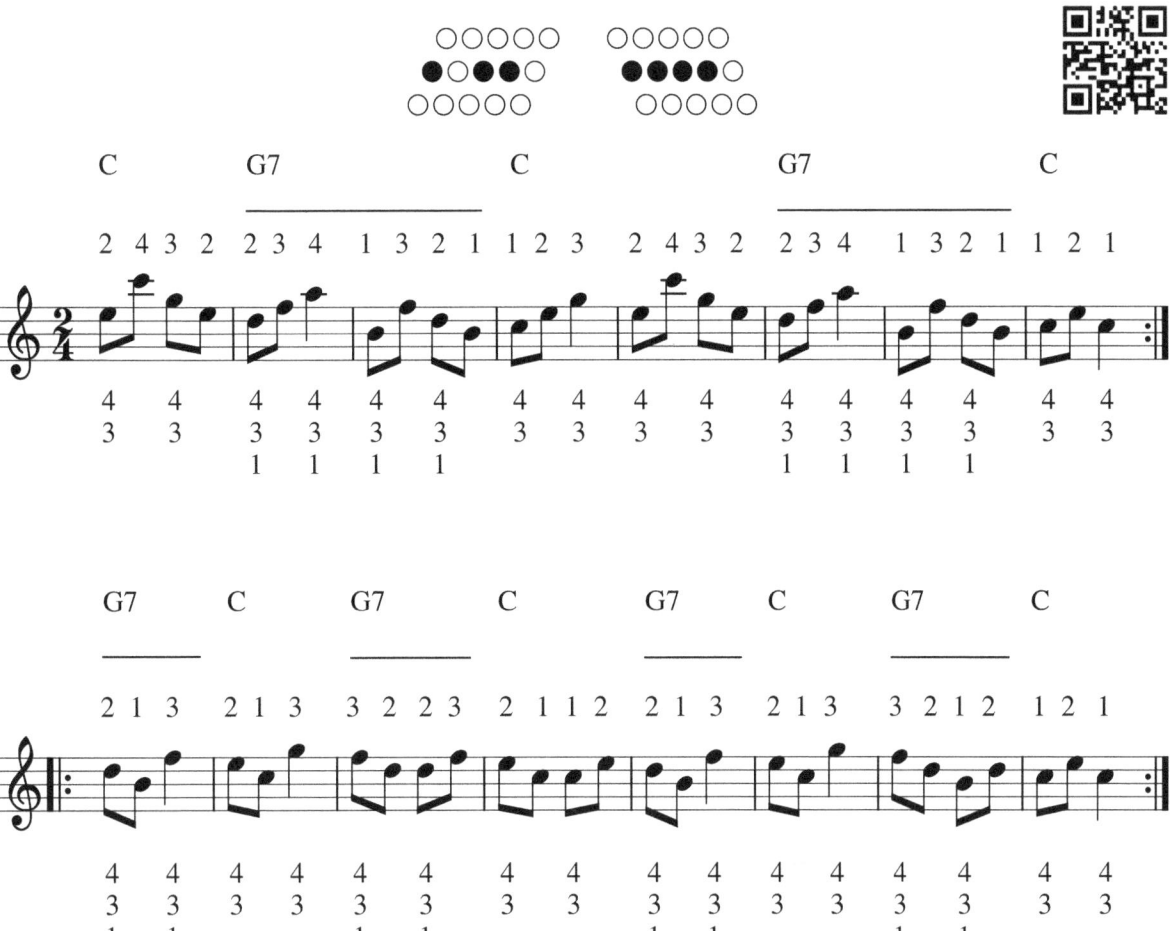

In the above tune, two chords are used C on the push and G7 on the pull, the chord being used is determined by the bellows direction of the melody. This idea of a two-chord vamp is developed in the following three tunes. Before exploring these tunes, we will first briefly consider the technique of this vamp alone. This two-chord vamp is simple and useful to begin with for several reasons:

- Both chords use the exact same buttons- one shape will give you a C chord on the push and a G7 on the pull, there is no need to change finger positions to find each chord.
- The chord used is decided by bellows direction of the melody, once you have set up the left-hand vamp in the correct rhythm, it essentially fits itself and you can focus on the melody.
- This basic principle can be applied to numerous tunes in the key of C.

The basic chord shapes that you need for this vamp are outlined below, both chords are played using buttons 1, 3 and 4 on the C row- this shape will give a C on the push and a G7 on the pull.

This vamp is based around alternation between the bottom note of this chord shape and the top two notes of this chord shape as indicated below- this is sometimes referred to as om-pahing.

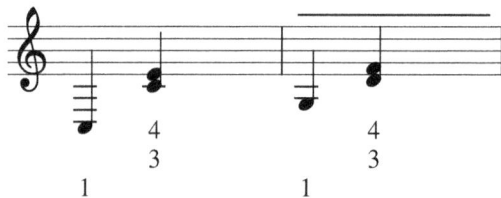

Now try it in rhythm:

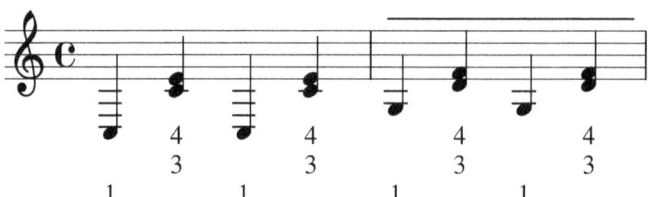

To fit this vamp into tunes, it is often best to play this vamp with shorter note values and a gap between the bass note and the chord as shown below:

Now try it in a few different time signatures, here it is in 3/4 or waltz time:

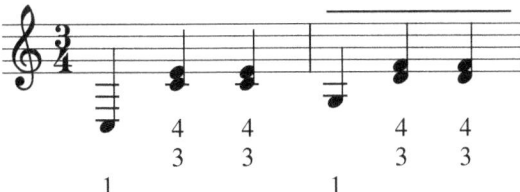

6/8 or jig time is a little more complex; a bar of 6/8 is made up of 6 quaver beats which are broken down into two lots of three quavers.

For each of these three quavers, you need to place a bass note on the first of the three and a chord on the third of the three, with a gap in the vamp for the middle of the three quavers.

A vamp in 6/8 can be shown through the following diagram, the top row shows the 6 quaver beats to a bar, the bottom row shows how the vamp fits within this (B= bass note; x= gap in vamp; C= chord).

1	2	3	4	5	6
B	x	C	B	x	C

Expressed in music it would look like this:

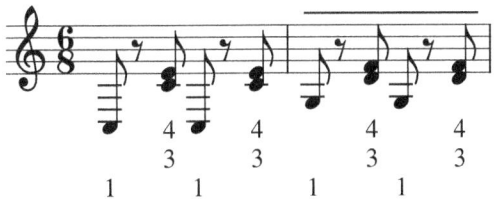

9/8 or slip-jig time, is essentially an extension of the 6/8 rhythm above, the vamp in 9/8 would look like this:

Tunes 2.2 and 2.3 both use variants of the vamp shown above in Waltz time. Tune 2.4, Tyroler Waltzer, also builds on the two-chord vamp, although using a slightly different chord shape, nevertheless the basic principle remains the same.

Tune 2.2

Minasi Waltz Number 7

Difficulty Level 2

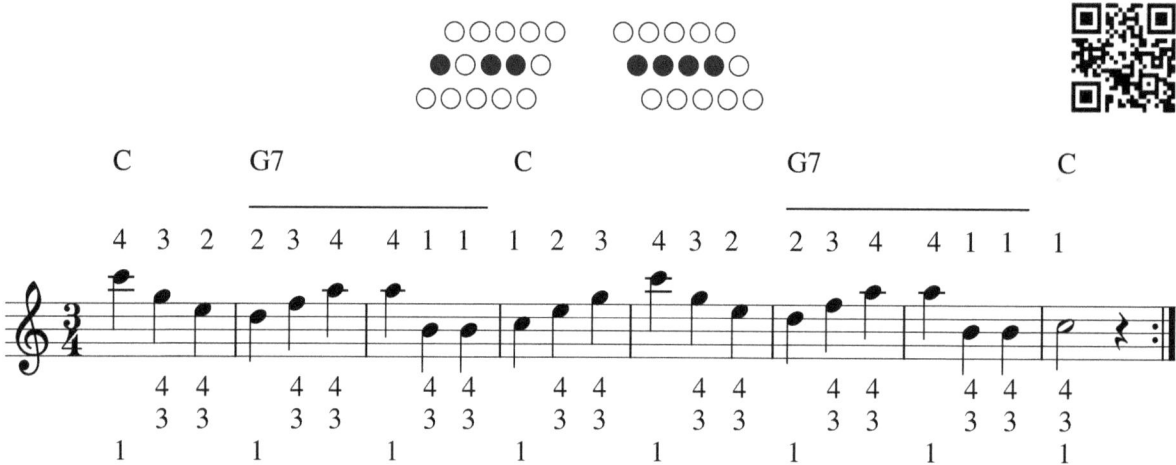

Tune 2.3

Waltz

Difficulty Level 2

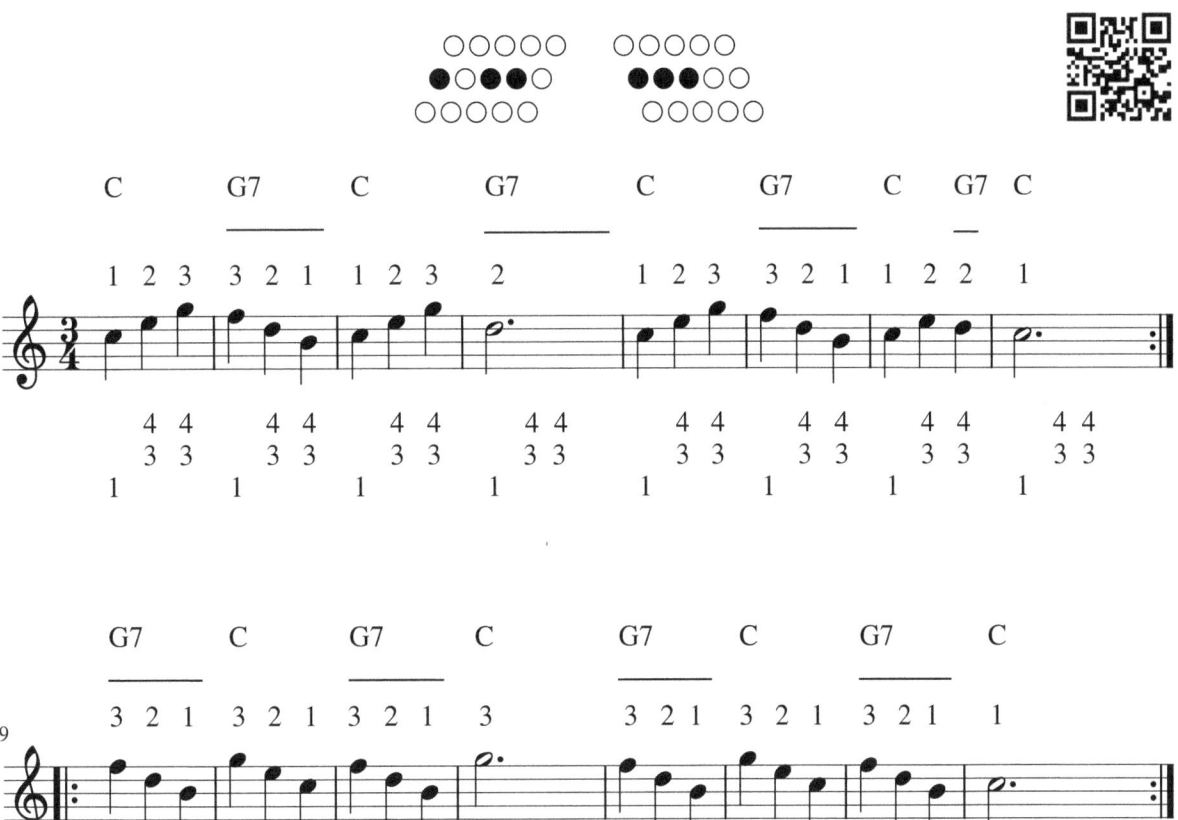

Tyroler Waltzer

Difficulty Level 3

The two-chord approach can be a simple and effective way to provide accompaniment to tunes many in C, however, the use of additional chords can often provide more pleasing accompaniments.

An effective way to provide accompaniment in any key is to use a technique known as the 'three chord trick'. The three chord trick uses chords I, IV and V in the relevant key; in the case of C, these chords would be C, F and G. Finding comfortable shapes for the three chord trick and practicing changing between these chords is a very useful first step when beginning with this technique- often once you have found these basic chord shapes, they can be applied to countless other tunes in the same key.

For the three-chord trick in C, these are my recommended home positions for the chords of C, F and G.

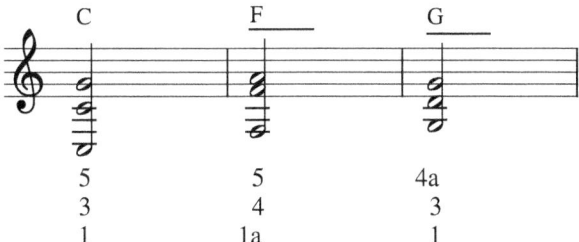

These three chords form the basis of the accompaniment to both of the following four tunes; however, you will notice that a few deviations from this basis are incorporated.

Tune 2.5

Westwood Park

Difficulty Level 3

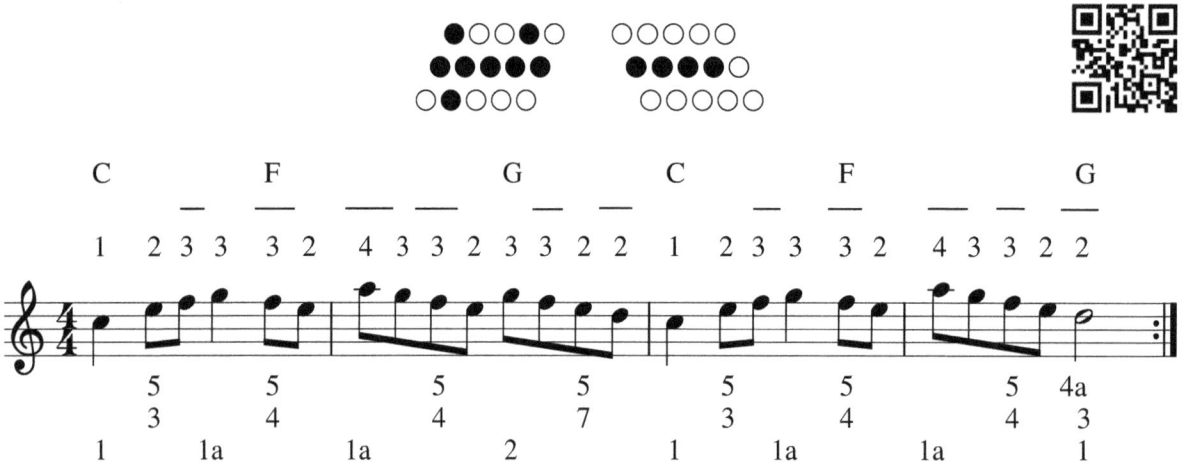

Tune 2.6

Litchfield Races

Difficulty Level 3

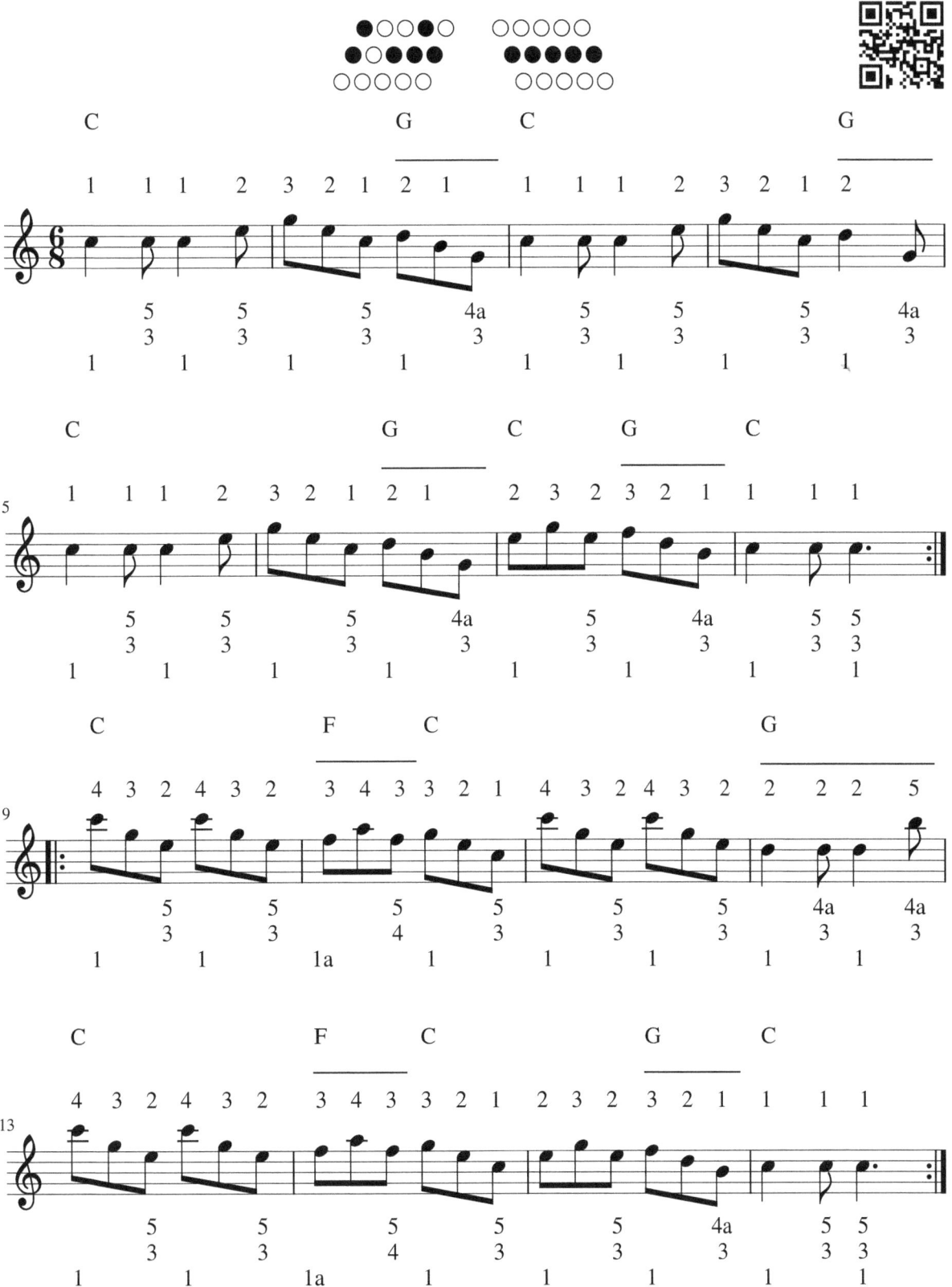

Tune 2.7

Lady Cathcart

Difficulty Level 3

Tune 2.8

The Exile

Difficulty Level 3

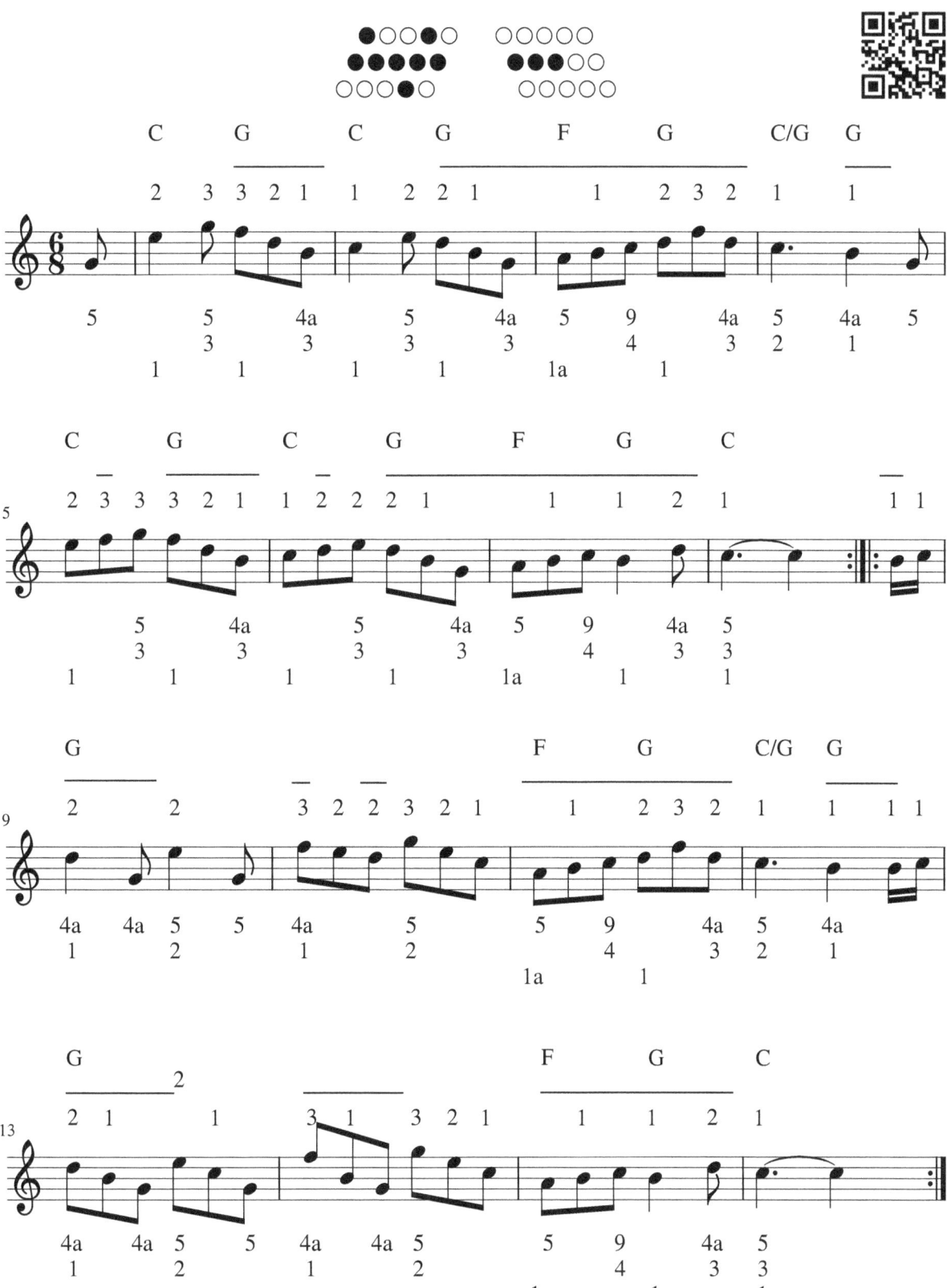

Tunes in G

Tunes in the key of G can create challenges for adding chordal accompaniment, often tunes will need to be played an octave higher than written to allow space for accompaniment under tunes, or else extensive row crossing will be required. Before exploring vamps in the key of G, we will first think about the home chord shapes for the three-chord trick in G.

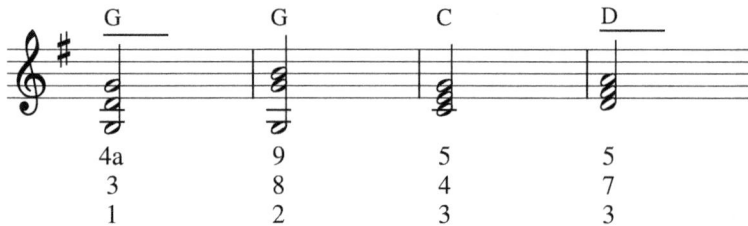

You will notice that there are two different shapes for the G chord- one on the pull and one on the push- these different chords shapes are each suited to their own situations as dictated by the tune. As before, try moving between the chords above as an exercise.

Tunes 2.9 and 2.10 are played in the higher octave, meaning the entire melody can fit comfortably on the right hand, in both cases the tunes have been transposed an octave higher than originally written to achieve this.

Tune 2.9

The Birmingham March

Difficulty Level 4

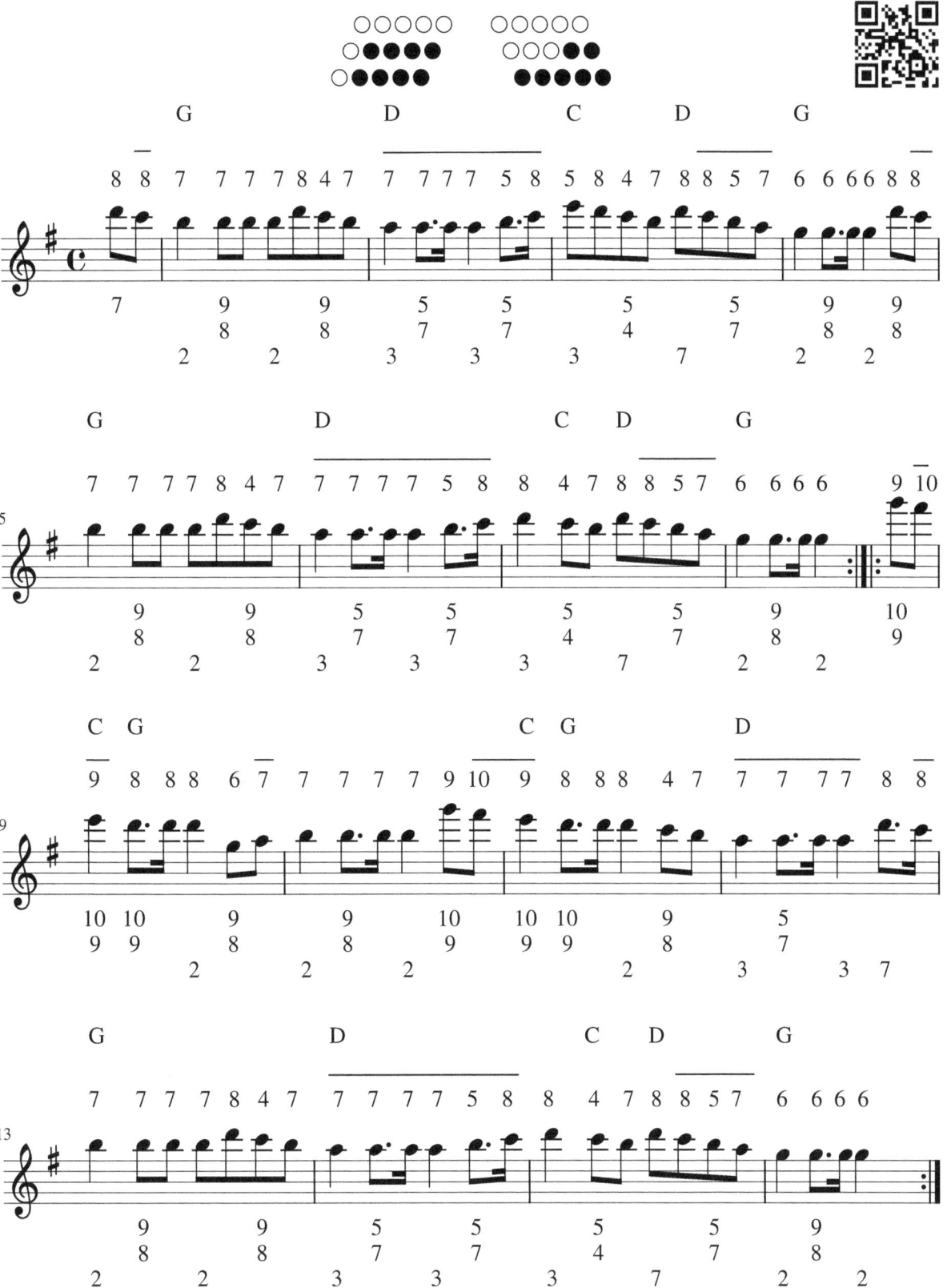

Tune 2.10

The Labarynth

Difficulty Level 4

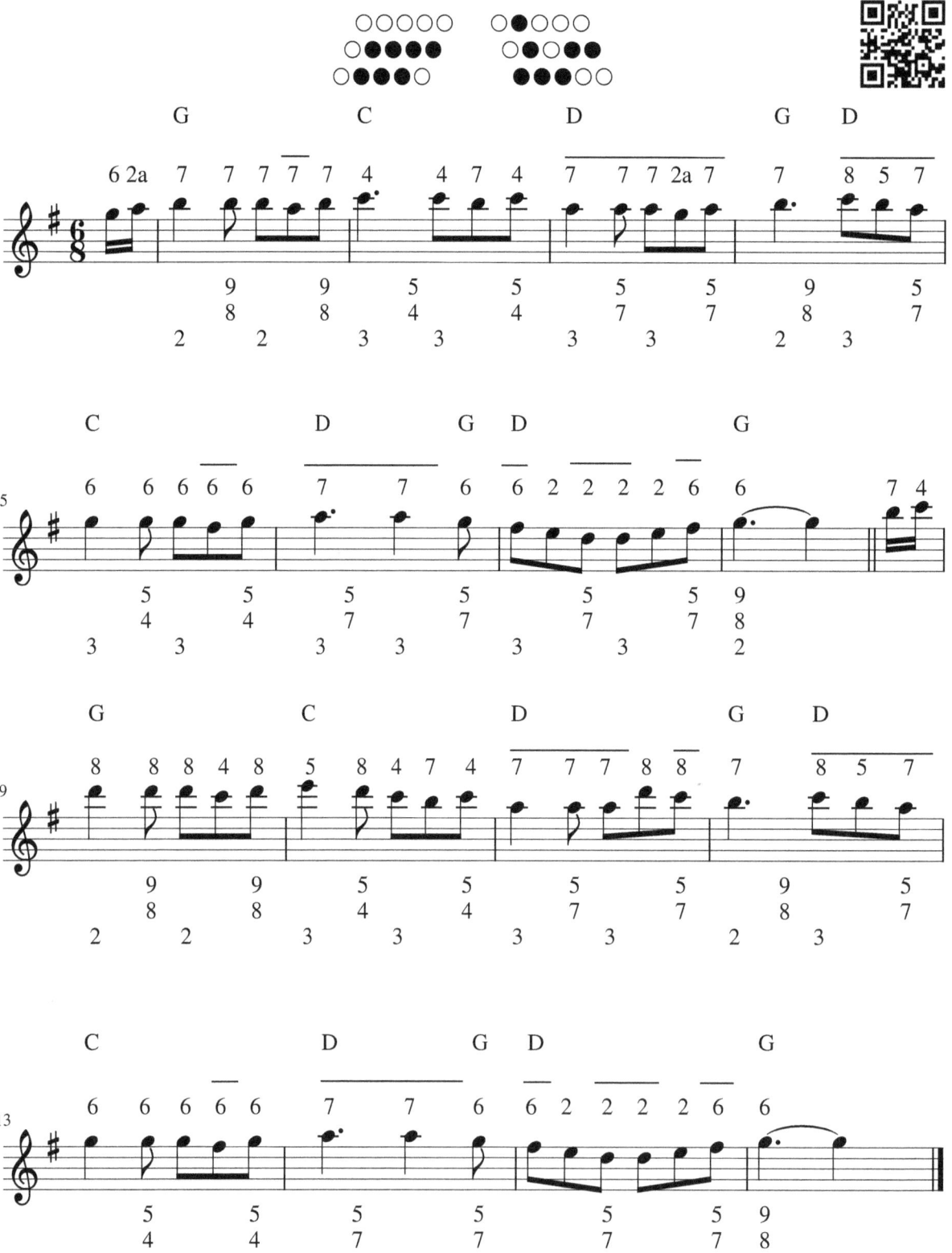

Tune 2.11

Since Tekeli is written in the higher register, there is no need to transpose it up an octave.

Tekeli

Difficulty Level 4

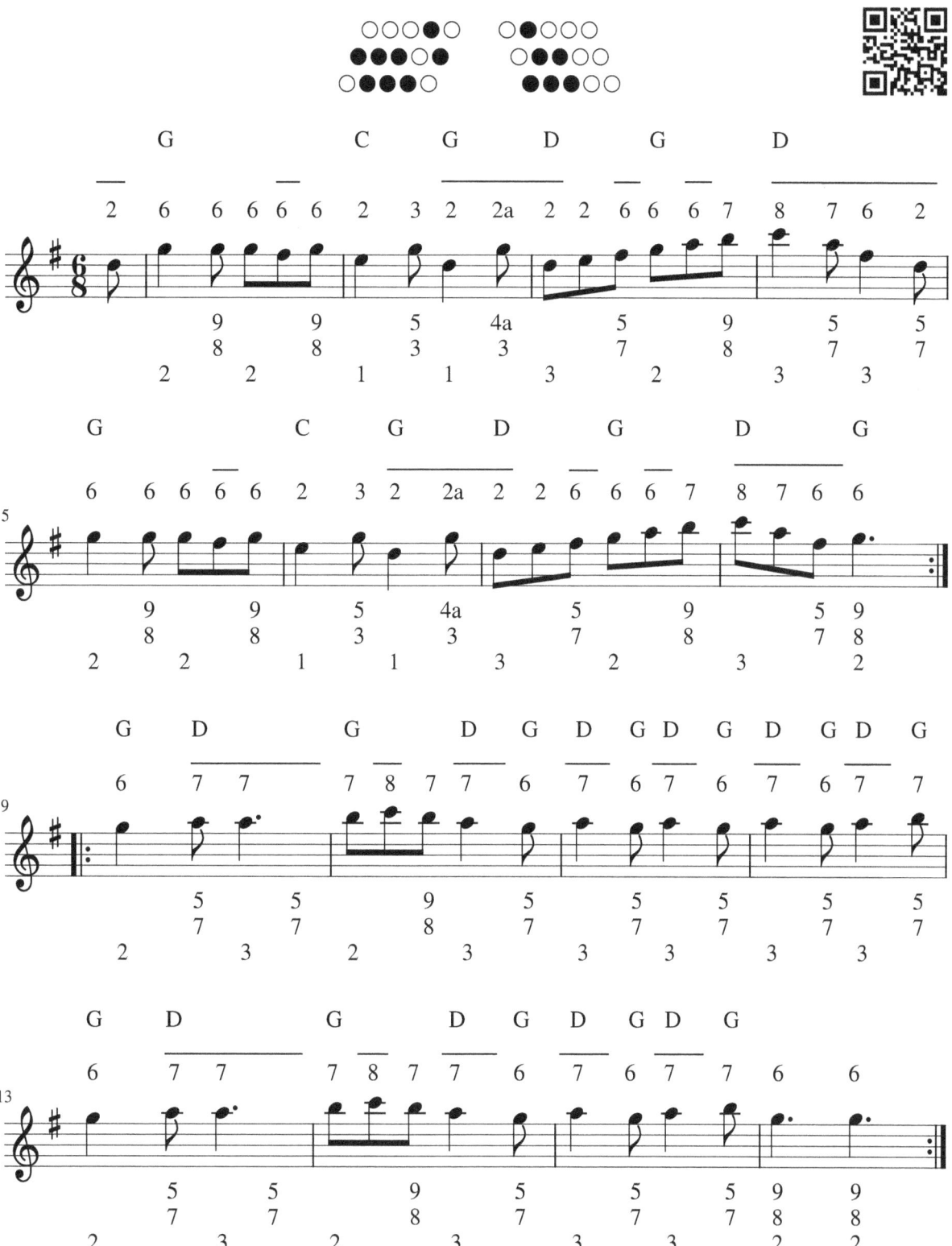

Sometimes, tunes will not suit being played in a higher octave. With a little bit of row crossing, tunes can be played with accompaniments in the lower octave in G. These final tunes explore this approach to playing in the chordal style in G.

Tune 2.12

Honey Moon

Difficulty Level 4

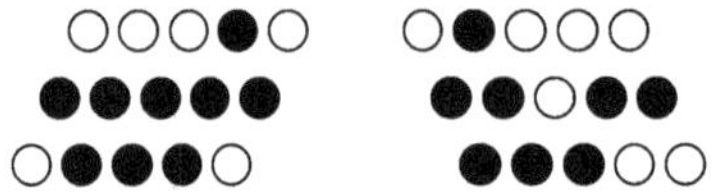

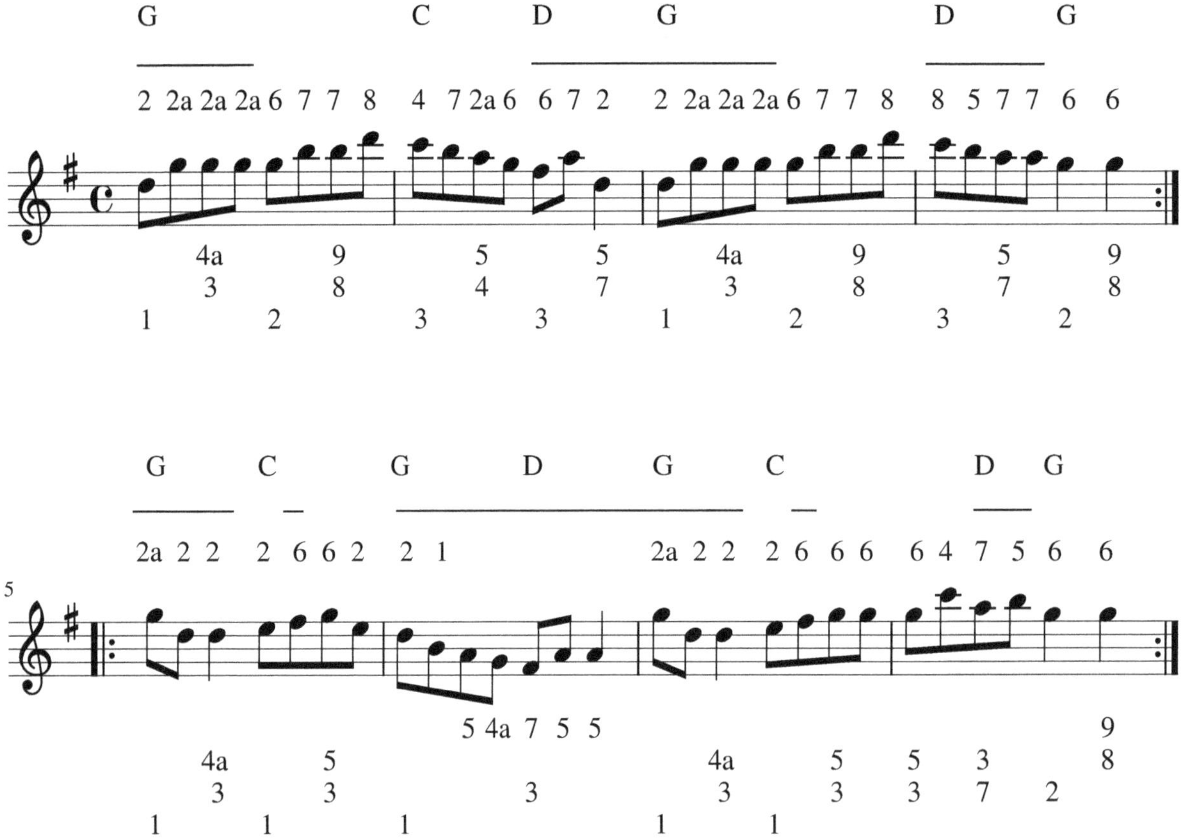

Tune 2.13

Paddy Wack

Difficulty Level 4

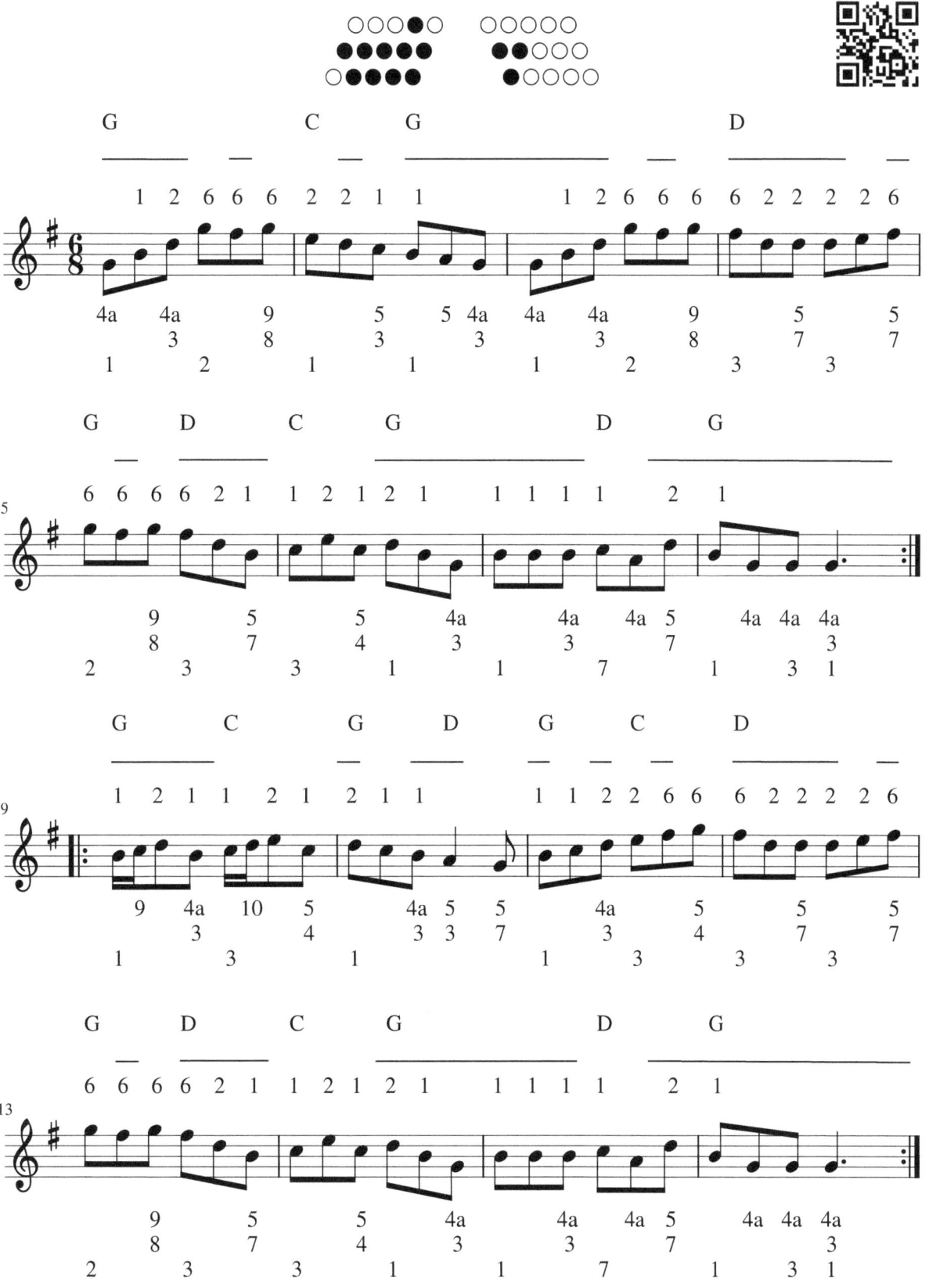

Tune 2.14

Frogmore Farm

Difficulty Level 4

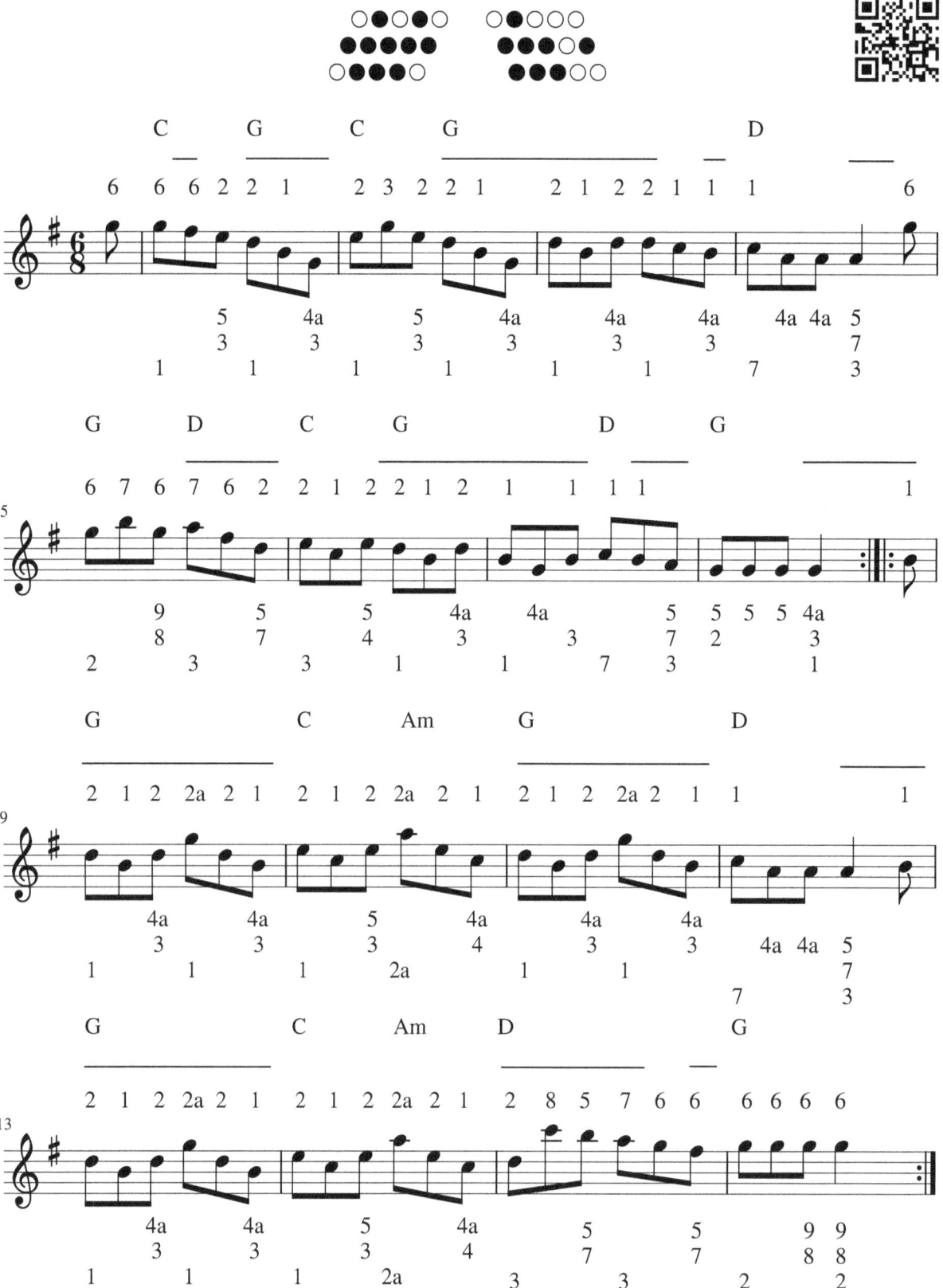

Tune 2.15

Miss Gayton's Hornpipe

Difficulty Level 4

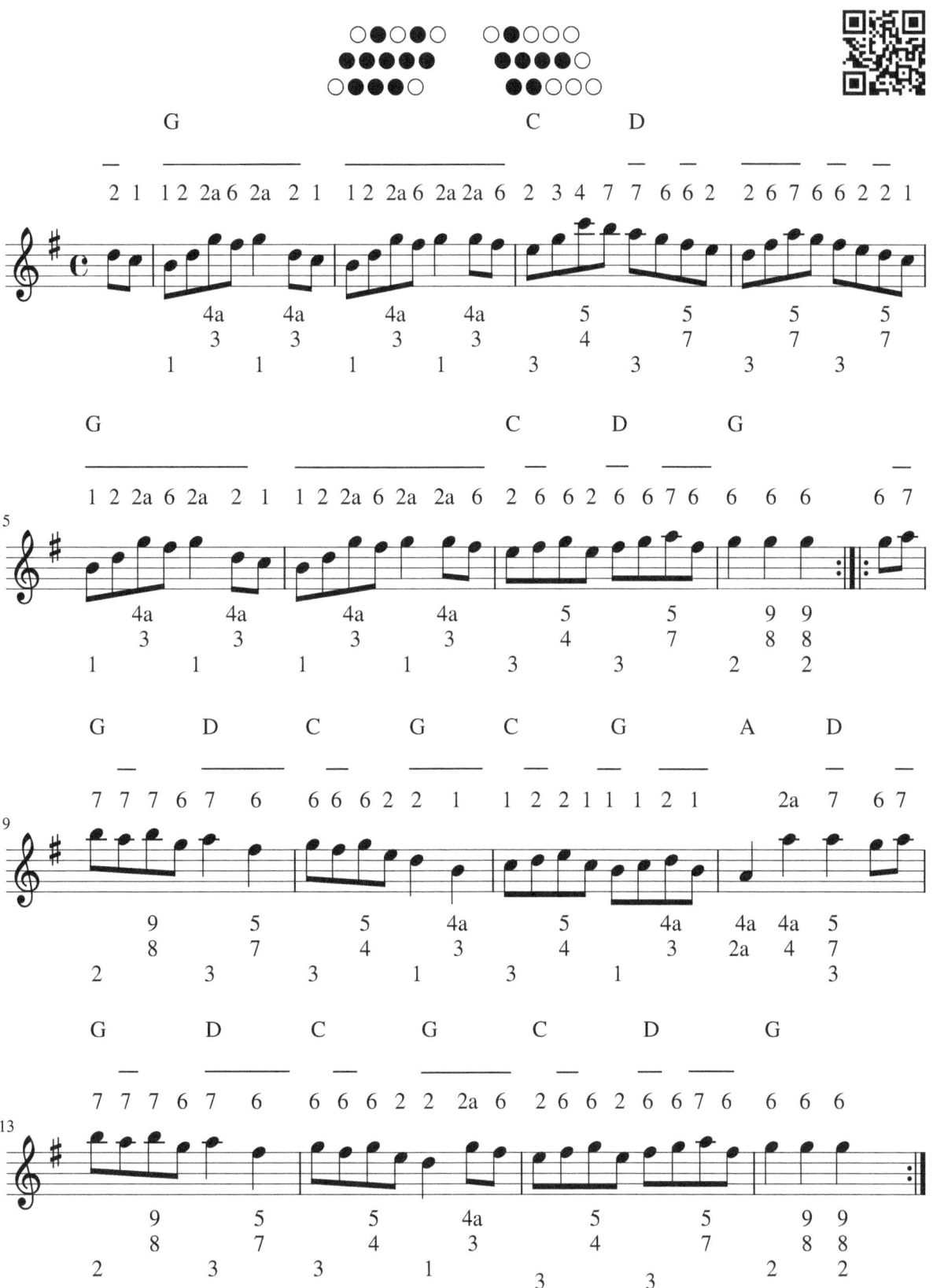

Concluding remarks

Through this chapter you should now be comfortable with adding accompaniment to tunes in the two home keys, providing a great foundation for looking at chordal accompaniment in new keys in the following chapter.

The idea of the 'three chord trick' in C and G can give you the basis for accompanying just about any tune in these two keys, and as you play more tunes in this style, you should get a feeling for where these chords should fall and thus you will be able to craft your own accompaniments.

As a starter exercise for crafting your own accompaniments, try taking the two chord C and G7 vamp from the opening of this chapter and applying it to some of the tunes in C from chapter one- that vamp can be effectively applied to tunes 1.1-1.5 using just the chord shapes and rhythms explored on pages 81-83.

Chapter 3: New keys

In this chapter we will look at playing in new keys outside of the home keys of C and G- beginning first with single note tunes and then introducing chordal accompaniment to some of these keys.

The key of D

The key of D features in some historical concertina tutors and is common in most folk music played today. To play in D, cross rowing is required. Exercises 3.1 and 3.2 show the fingering for a D major scale in both the lower and upper octaves.

Exercise 3.1

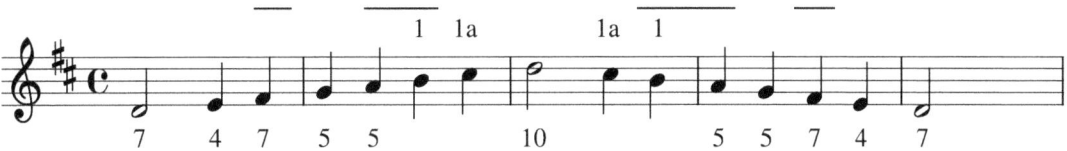

Exercise 3.2

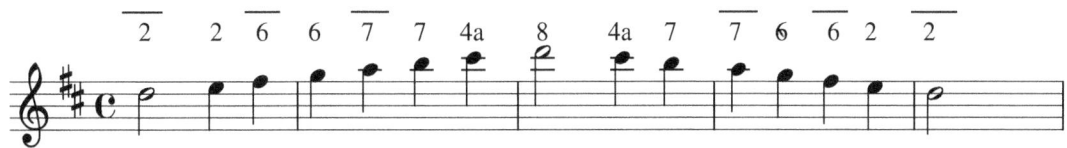

Now try the following single note tunes in D.

Tune 3.1

Ellingham Assembly

Difficulty Level 3

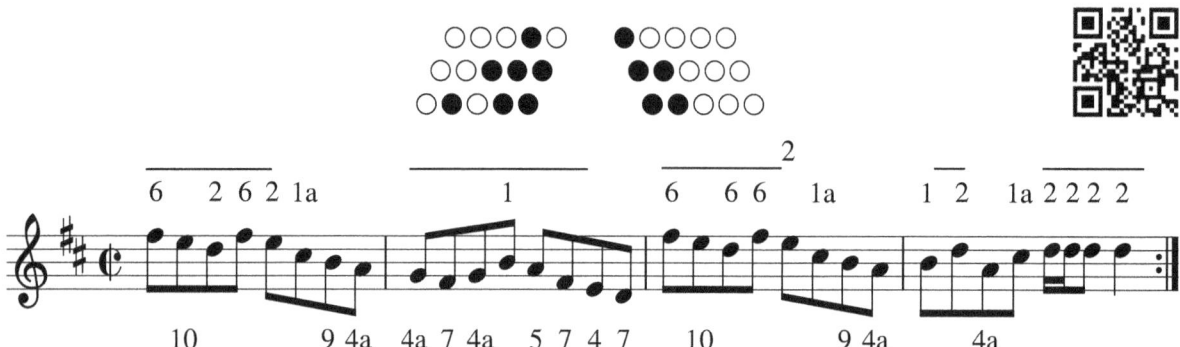

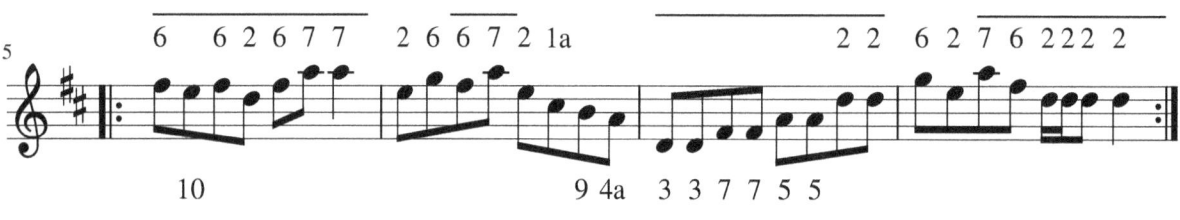

Tune 3.2

Now or Never

Difficulty Level 3

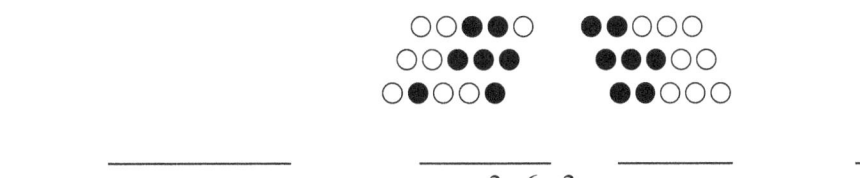

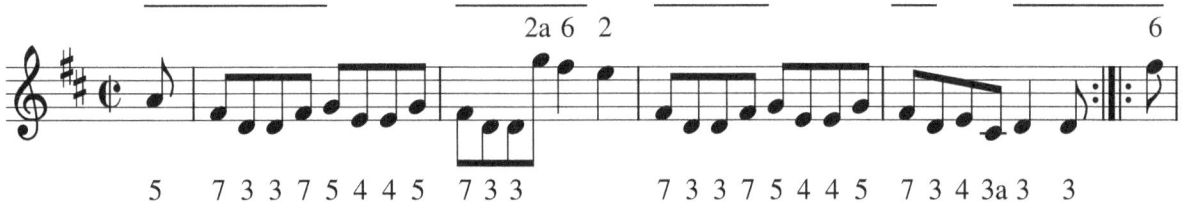
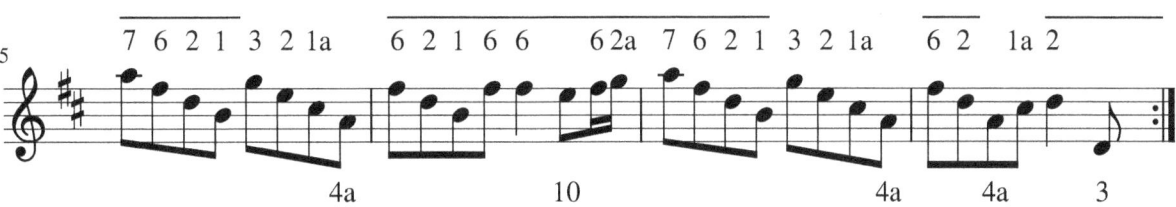

Using the accidental row

We have already ventured onto the accidental row for the purposes of row crossing in the home keys and to play the C# needed for tunes in D. The following tunes feature other chromatic notes, requiring further use of the accidental row.

Tune 3.3

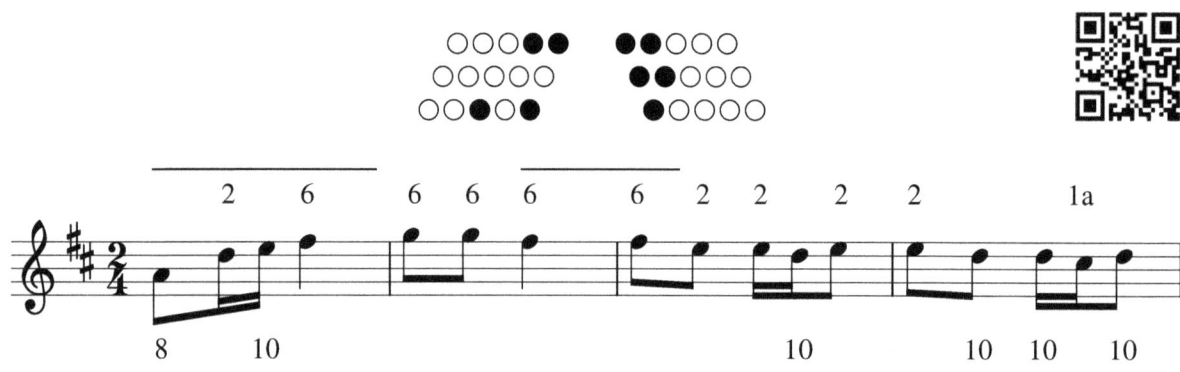

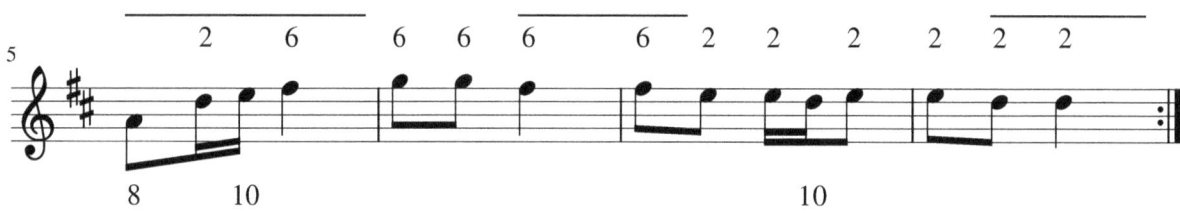

Tune 3.4

The Philosopher's Jigg

Difficulty Level 3

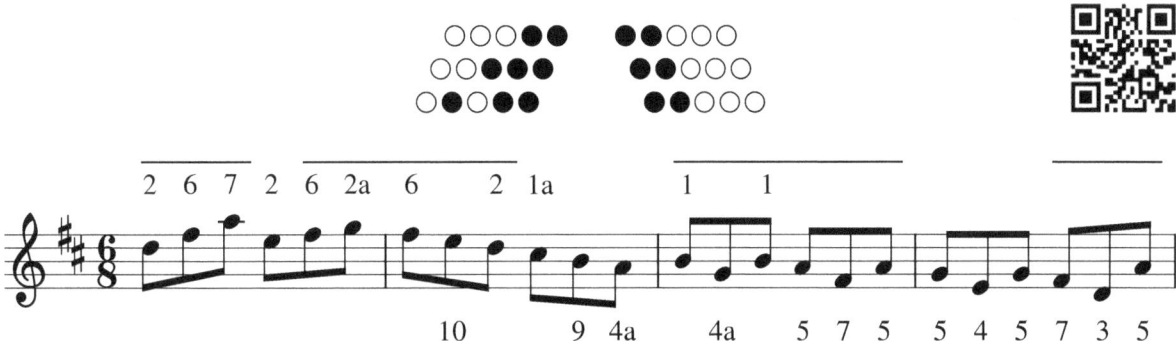

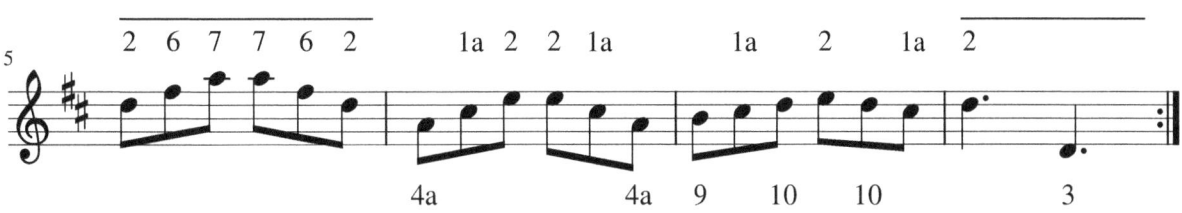

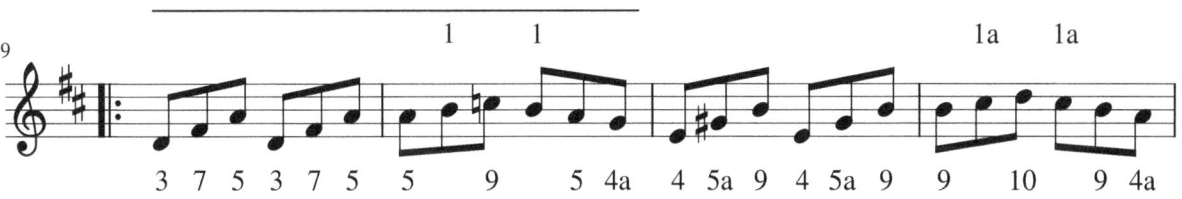

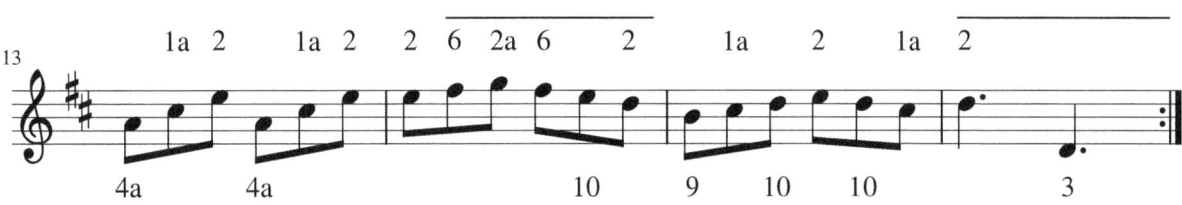

The key of A

The key of A is another important key for both historical and modern concertina playing. Exercise 3.3 is a one octave A major scale and is followed by tune 3.5, a jig in A.

Exercise 3.3

Tune 3.5

Trip to London

Difficulty Level 3

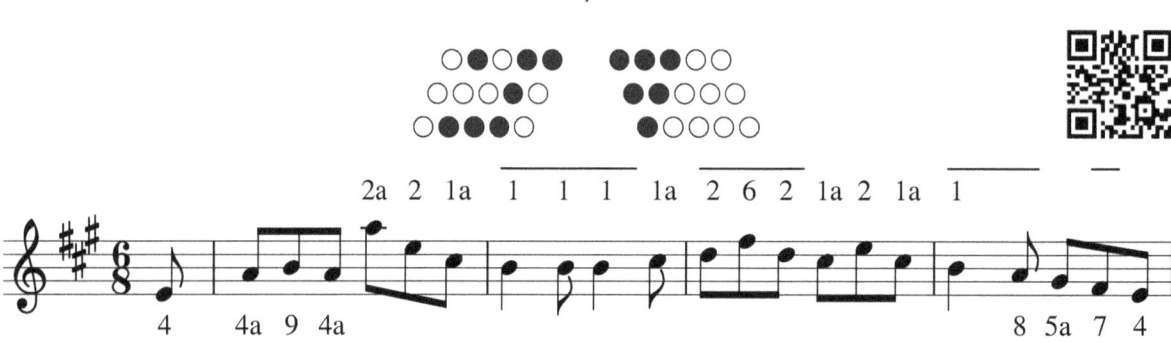

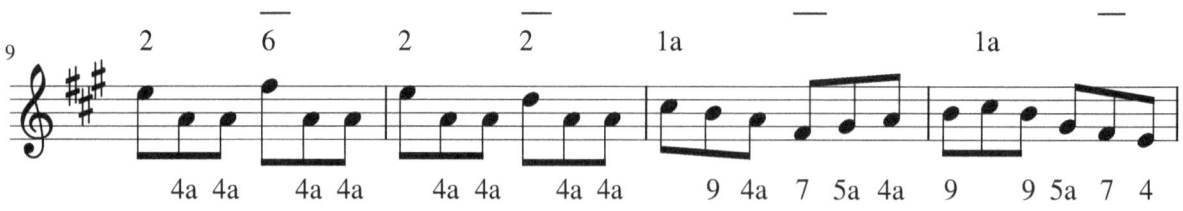

The key of F

The key of F is common in historical concertina tutors, but not hugely common in folk music today, though it does fit nicely on the C/G Anglo concertina. Exercises 3.4 is a two octave F major scale and is followed by tune 3.6, a hornpipe in F.

Exercise 3.4

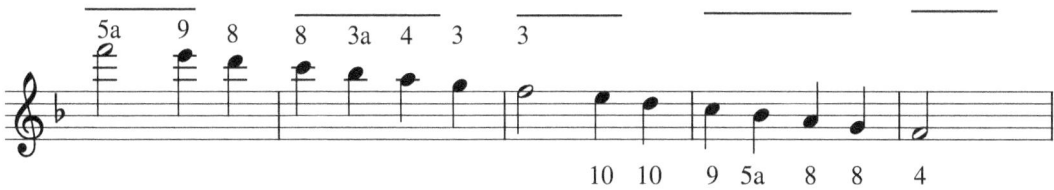

Tune 3.6

Saxon Hornpipe

Difficulty Level 3

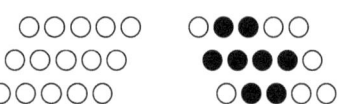 

Tunes in other modes/minor scales

Having looked at three new major keys, we will now look briefly at some other types of scales. In conventional music the two main scales are the major scale and the minor scale, the minor scale will be explored briefly at the end of this section. In most folk music, modal scales are used instead of classical minor scales.

In folk music of the British Isles, there alongside the major and minor scales, the Aeolian, Dorian and Mixolydian modes are sometimes found.

Below are a series of modal scales in the Aeolian, Dorian and Mixolydian modes. Each mode is shown in the three most common key signatures for British folk music. After this there is one tune for each mode.

Aeolian Mode

The Aeolian mode is also known as the natural minor scale. Below are Aeolian scales on A (no sharps), E (one sharp) and B (two sharps).

Aeolian on A

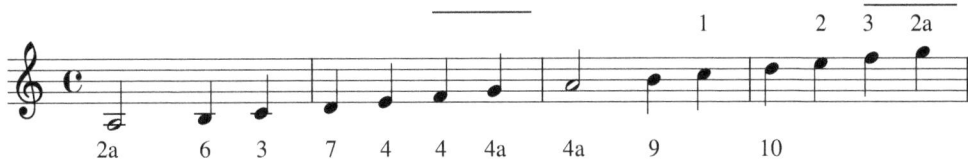

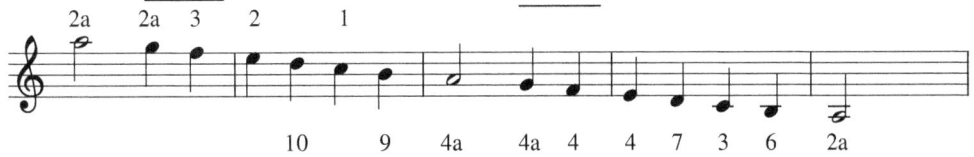

Aeolian on E

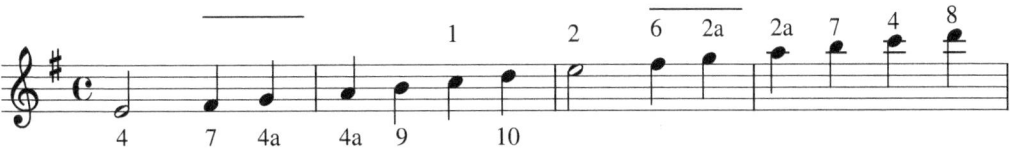

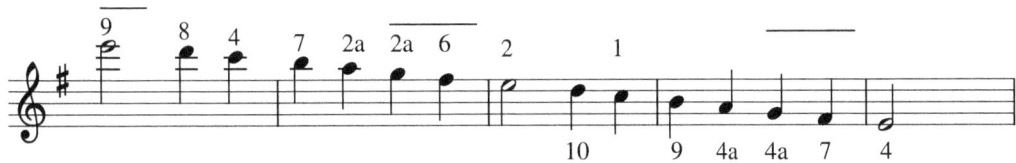

Aeolian on B

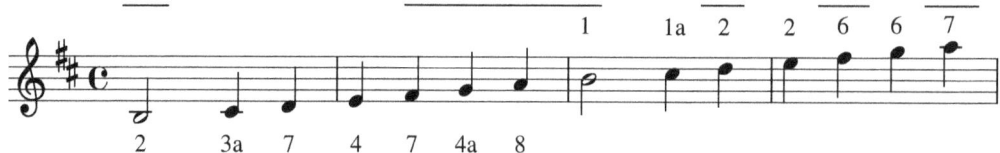

Dorian Mode

The Dorian mode is another minor mode. It is similar to the Aeolian mode; however, the 6th degree of the scale is sharpened. Below are Dorian scales on D (no sharps), A (one sharp) and E (two sharps).

Dorian on D

Dorian on A

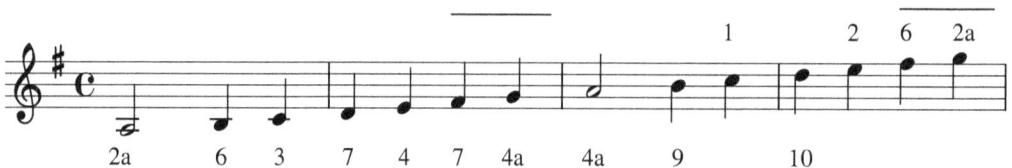

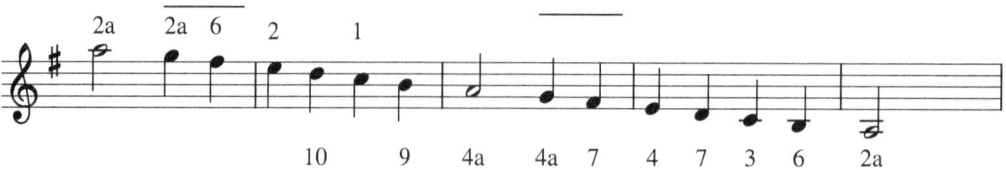

Dorian on E

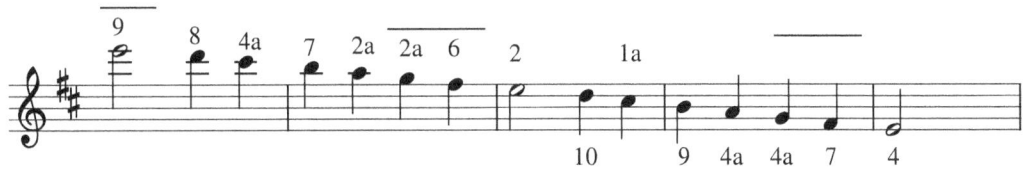

Mixolydian Mode

The Mixolydian mode falls under the category of a major mode. It differs from the standard major scale in having a flattened 7th. Below are Mixolydian scales on G (no sharps), D (one sharp) and A (two sharps).

Mixolydian on G

Mixolydian on D

Mixolydian on A

Tunes 3.7-3.9 below demonstrate some of these modal scales above in practice. Take a Dance is in the B Aeolian mode; 3.8, The Unfortunate Cup of Tea is in the E Dorian mode; and 3.9 Wilkes's Wriggle is in the A Mixolydian mode.

Tune 3.7

Take a Dance

Difficulty Level 3

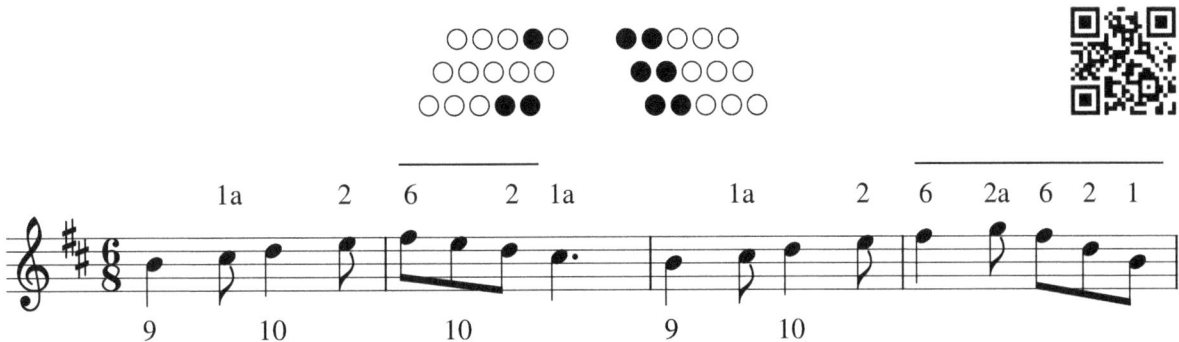

Tune 3.8

The Unfortunate Cup of Tea

Difficulty Level 3

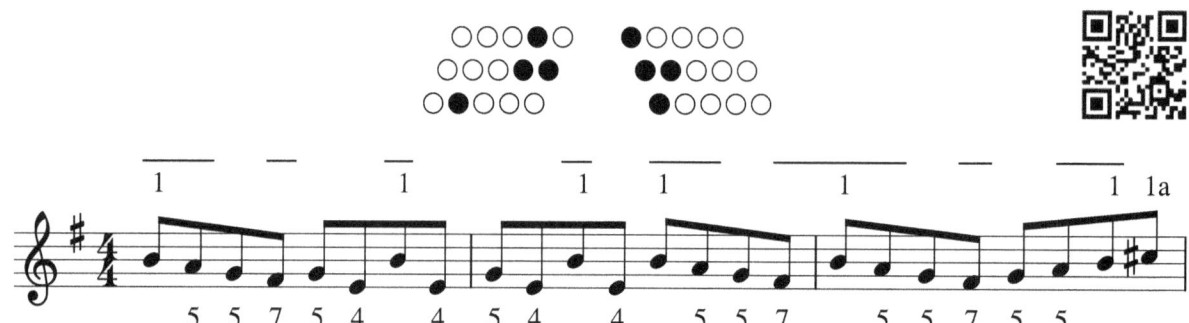

Tune 3.9

Wilkes's Wriggle

Difficulty: Level 3

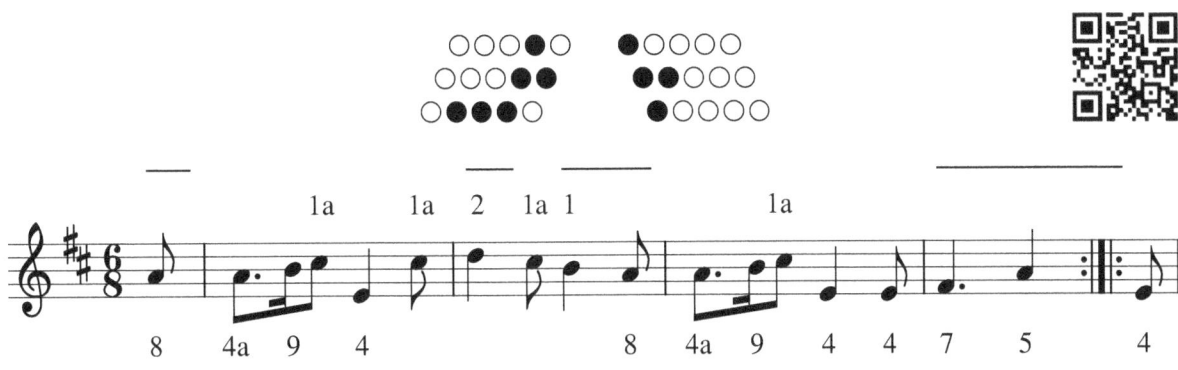

Harmonic and Melodic minors

Harmonic and melodic minor scales feature more commonly than modal scales in historic concertina tutors. These scales feature occasionally in traditional music and are prevalent in classical music. Below are harmonic and melodic minor scales in E (1 sharp).

You will notice that the E harmonic minor scale is almost identical to the Aeolian mode, however the 7th note in the scale is sharpened (in this case a D sharp).

E harmonic minor

The E melodic minor is essentially two scales- one scale ascending, another descending. The descending scale is identical to the E aeolian mode, for the ascending scale the 6th and 7th notes of the scale are sharpened (in this case a C sharp and a D sharp).

E melodic minor

Tune 3.10

The Fiddler's Jig uses the E melodic minor scale.

The Fiddler's Jig

Difficulty Level 3

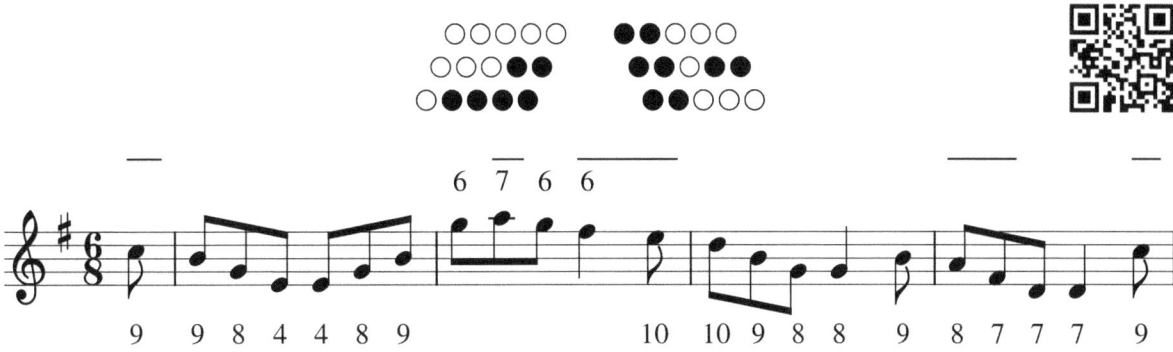

To conclude this chapter on exploring new keys, we will consider how to approach chordal accompaniment in some of these new keys.

Tunes 3.11-3.13 explore some ways in which chordal accompaniment can be added to tunes in D.

Tune 3.11

Welsh Fusiliers

Difficulty Level 4

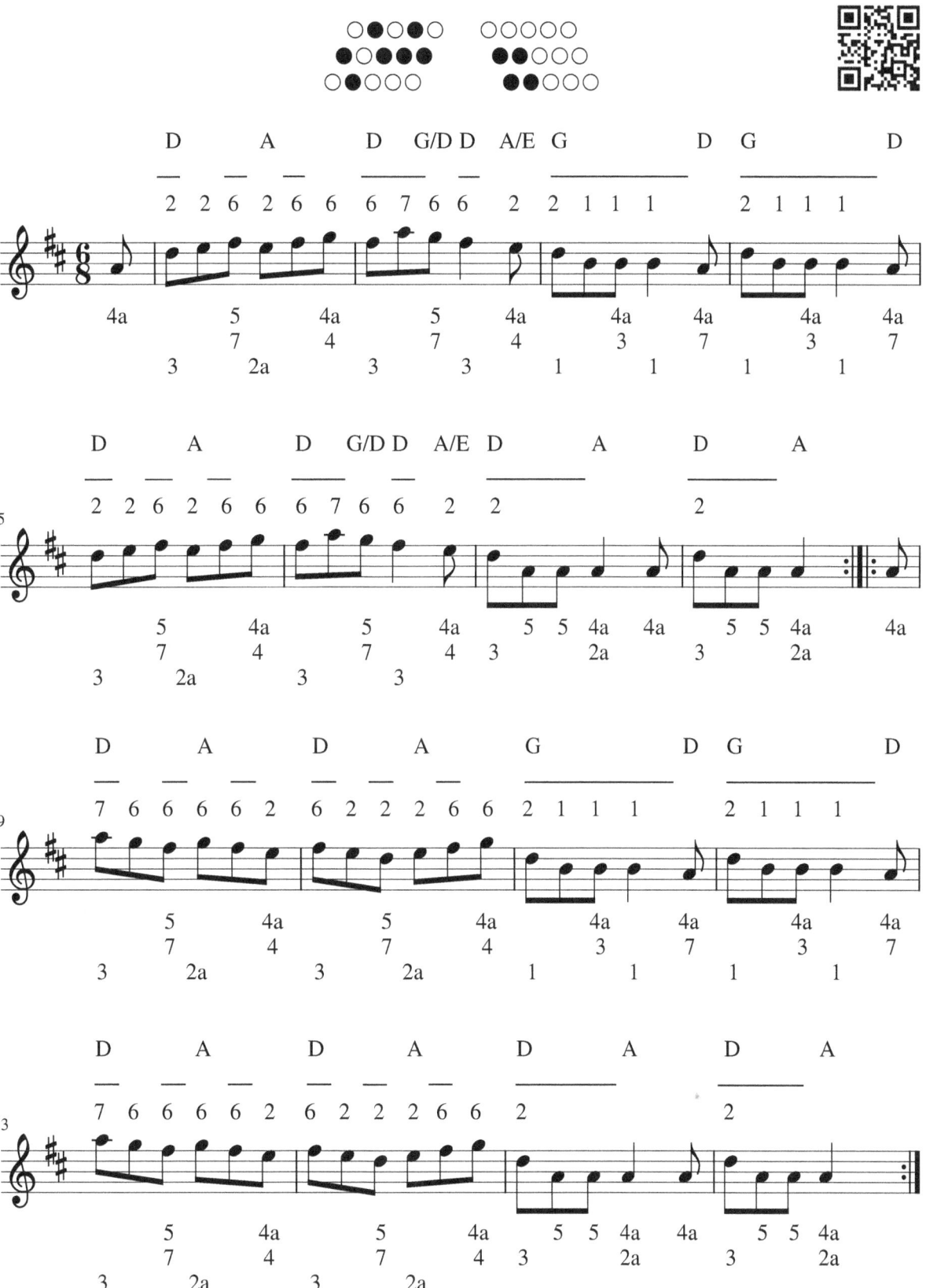

Tune 3.12

Cure of all Grief

Difficulty Level 4

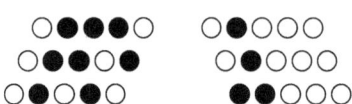

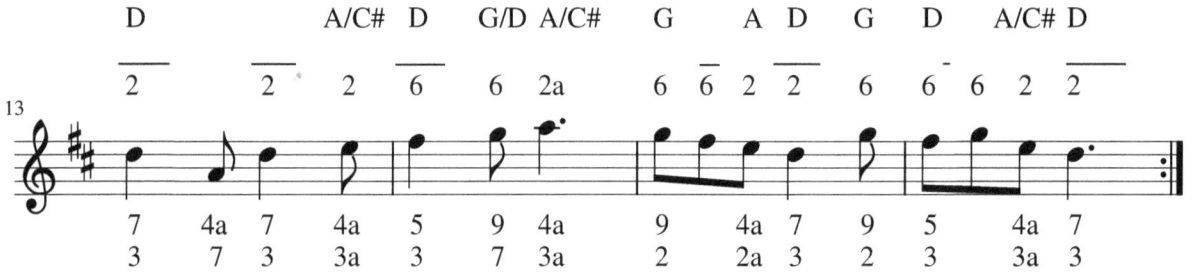

Tune 3.13

Harliquin Air

Difficulty Level 4

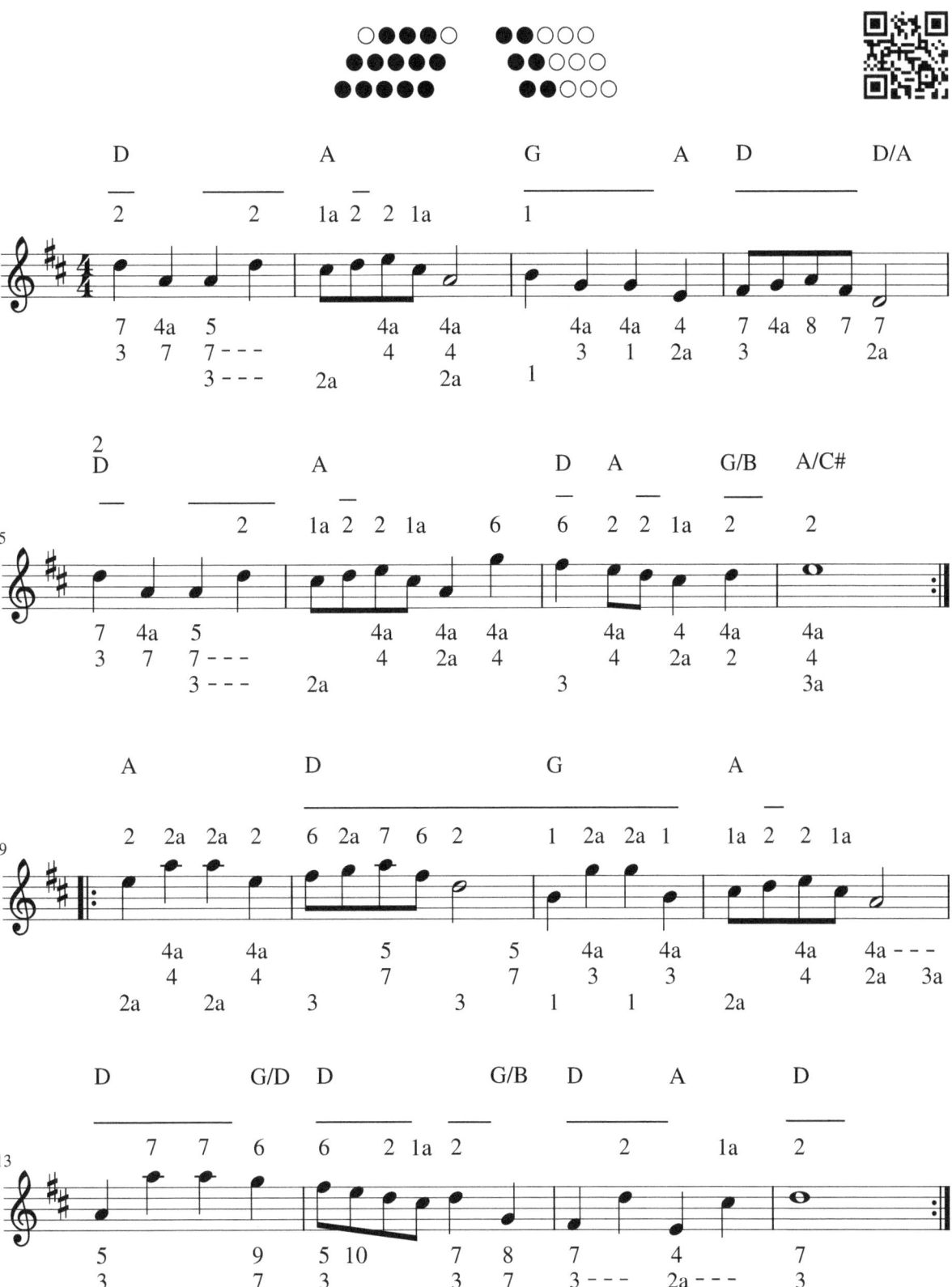

We will finish this chapter with a tune in E minor with chordal accompaniment.

Tune 3.14

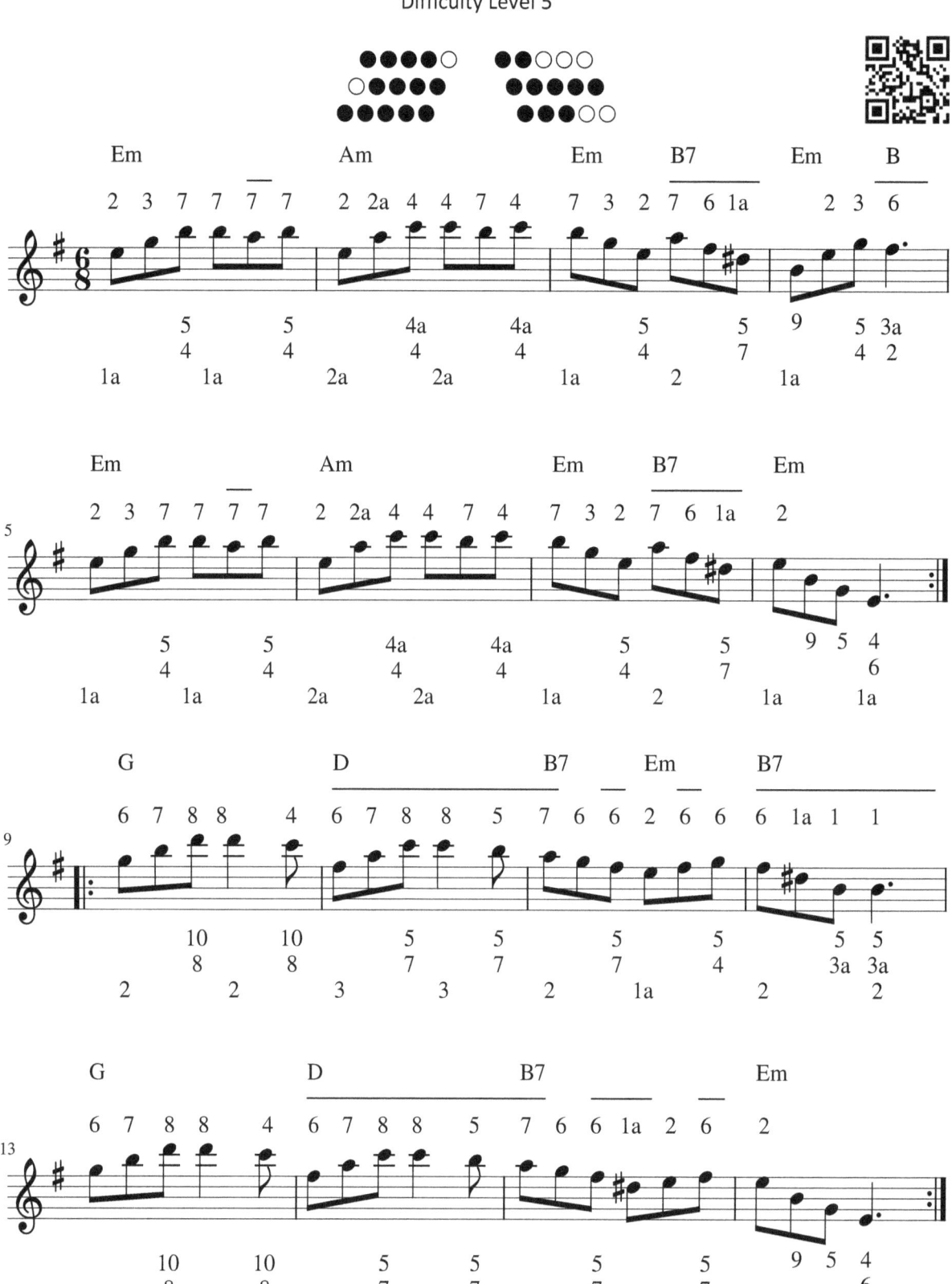

Through these first three chapters you should now be able to play tunes in some of the most common keys needed for traditional music. You should also be comfortable with providing chord vamps to tunes in a number of these keys. You may however have noticed that this vamping approach fits easier on some tunes in certain keys than others and that chordal playing outside of the home keys can be less formulaic and require more compromises. In fact, you may find that alternative approaches to accompaniment explored in the coming chapters may provide more satisfactory results outside of the home keys.

Chapter 4: Chordal Accompaniment

In the previous chapters, we have explored the idea of using chords to accompany your own playing, an alternate way of chordal concertina playing is to use the concertina to provide chordal accompaniment to other musicians or singers. The Anglo concertina has been used throughout its history to provide chordal accompaniment to singers or other instruments and this technique is useful for modern concertina players not just for providing accompaniments to songs or tunes but can also be a great exercise in finding chords and developing chordal vamps.

The material in this chapter provides a brief introduction to a useful and versatile, yet seldom discussed approach to Anglo concertina playing. When playing in an ensemble setting or if accompanying your own singing, the use of chordal accompaniment patterns is a very valuable tool to have in your concertina playing repertoire and I would fully recommend experimenting and exploring it further, trying out accompaniments for pieces in a range of keys, rhythms, and speeds.

Chord shapes

The following 'primary chords' are the main chords that you will need for chordal accompaniment on the Anglo concertina. These chords can be used to provide accompaniments in the keys of C, G and D along with their related minors and modes (the main keys you are likely to use in your concertina playing). You will recognise many of these shapes from the previous chapters.

Primary chords

Major

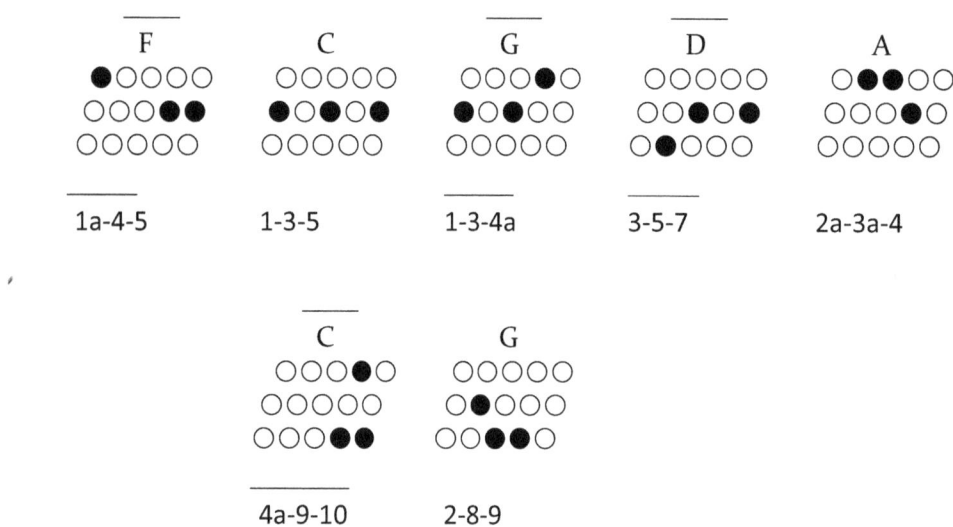

Minor

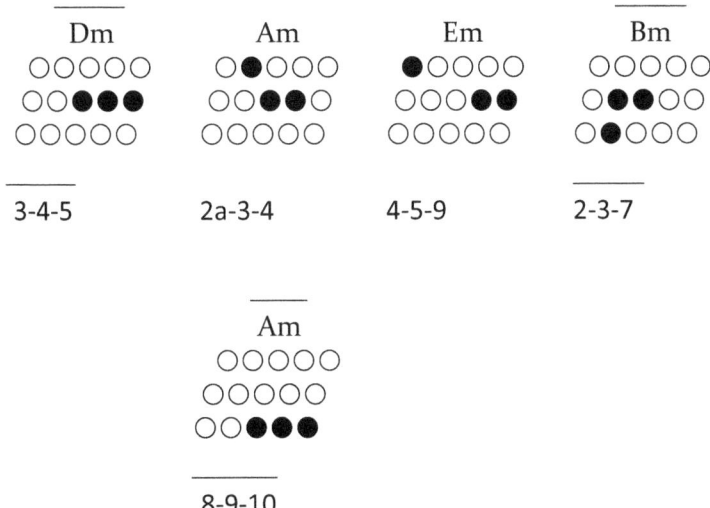

The following additional chords can be used to open up further possibilities for keys, using these (in some cases in conjunction with the primary chords above) you will be able to play additionally in the keys of Eb, Bb, F, A and E along with their related minors and modes.

Additional chords

Major

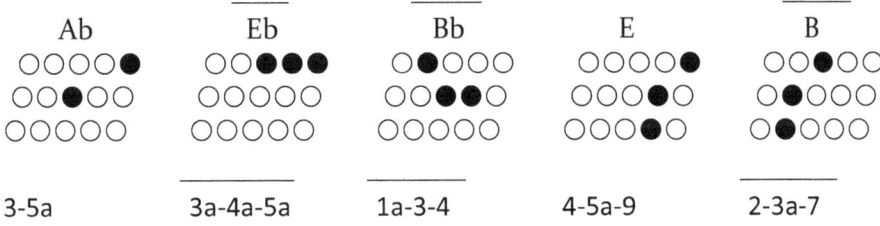

Minor

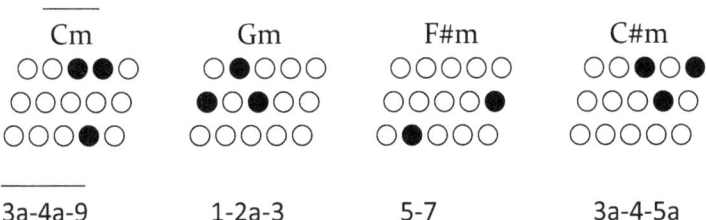

It is worth noting that the shapes above are not the only possible positions for these chords; all chords have numerous possible positions across the concertina keyboard.

The following exercises demonstrates some of the possible alternative positions for the chords of C and G. In the manner of the chordal vamps shown in the previous chapters, the exercise alternates between a bass note and a chord, however, each time a chord is played in this vamp, it appears in a different shape to the previous chord.

Exercise 4.1: Inversion exercise C

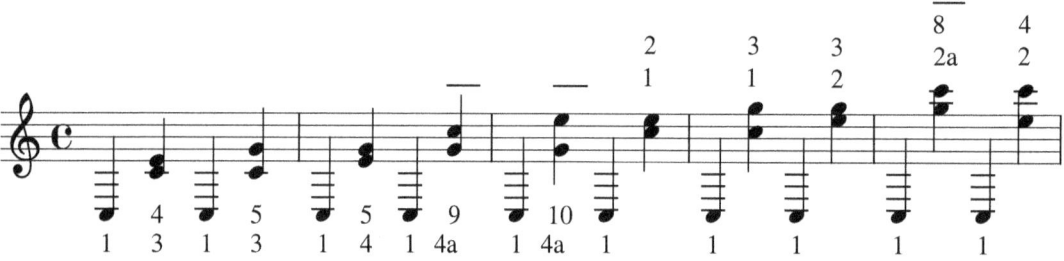

Exercise 4.2: Inversion exercise G

Now that you have a basic knowledge of chord shapes, try the following tunes. I have arranged these for two parts- the top line is the melody, the bottom line is a chordal accompaniment for the concertina- why not try playing these with a friend, the top line can be played on just about any melody instrument. Alternately, by following the links in the QR codes, you can play along to my own split screen recordings.

Tune 4.1

Union Waltz

Difficulty Level 2

Tune 4.2

The Buds of May

Difficulty Level 4

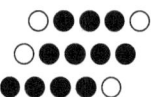 

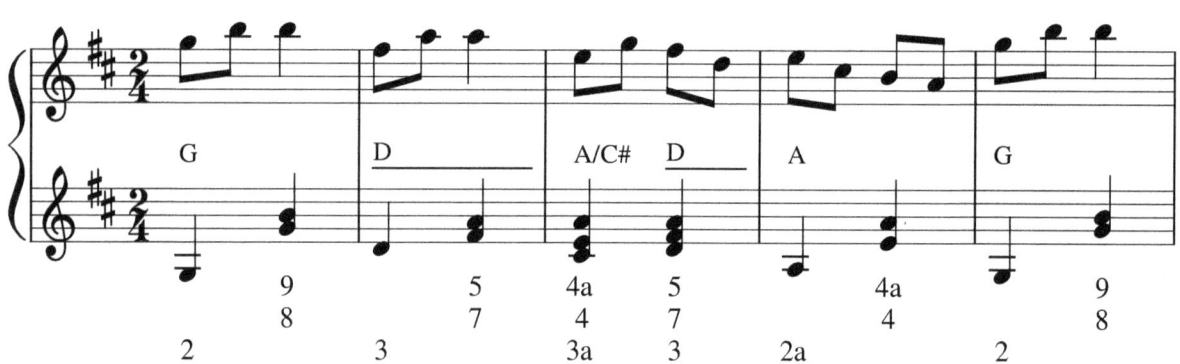

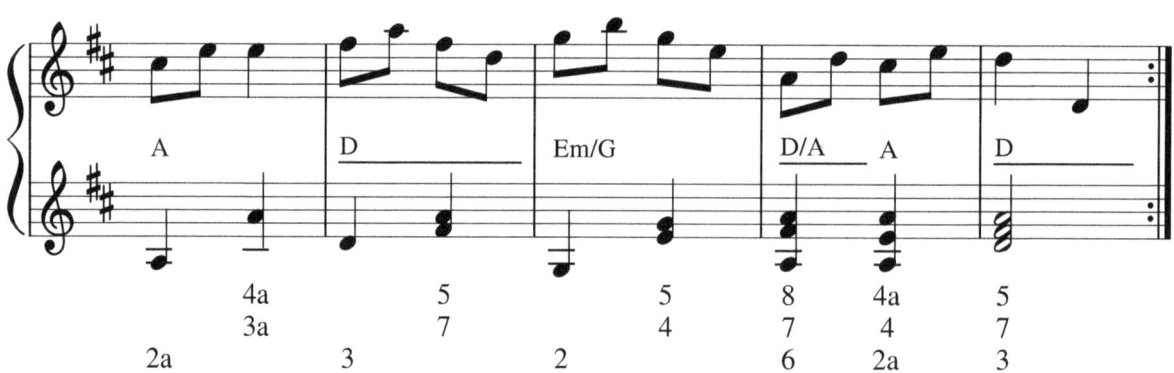

Tune 4.3

Spring's Waltz

Difficulty Level 4

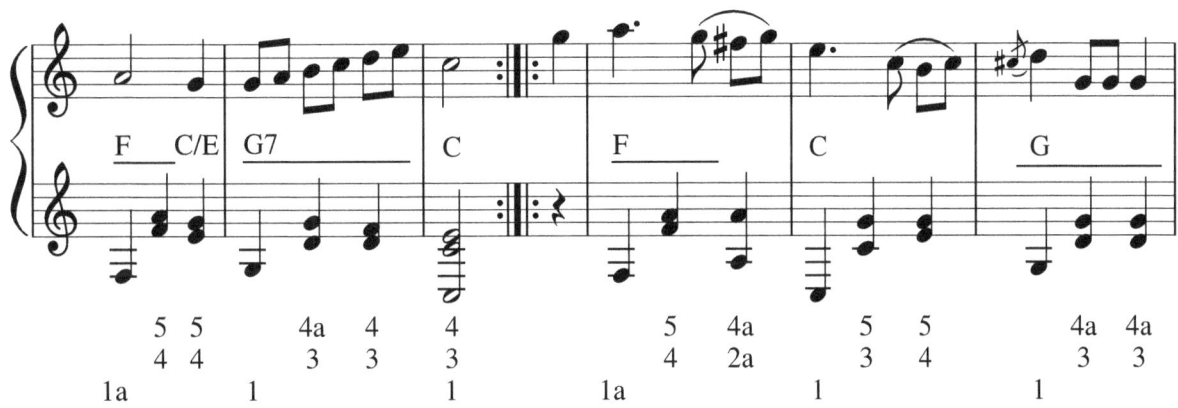

Tune 4.4

Freedom and Liberty

Difficulty Level 4

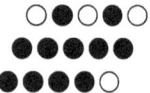 

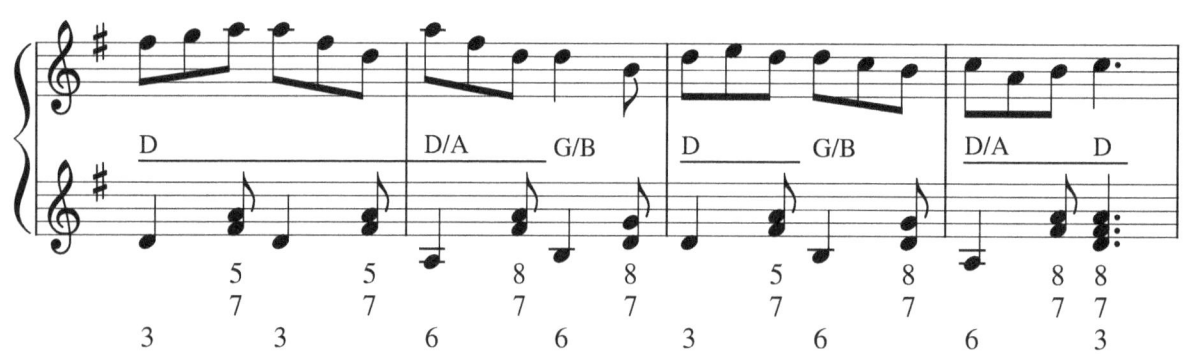

Tune 4.5

Rakish Highlandman

Difficulty Level 4

Anglo Concertina from Beginner to Master

Chapter 5: Playing in Octaves

The style of playing in octaves has been prevalent for much of the Anglo concertina's history with players across the world and remains popular with concertina players today. Dan Worrall's *House Dance* gives a full explanation of this style along with recorded examples and is a highly recommended text on the subject.

In the following chapter, we will work through the skills of playing in octaves in the keys of C, G and D through exercises and a tune for each key, there is also one modal tune. In the following chapter all of the tunes, along with exercise 5.2 are written as single notes, the octave doubling is shown through tablature.

Playing in octaves in the key of C

Below is an exercise for playing a C major scale in octaves:

Exercise 5.1

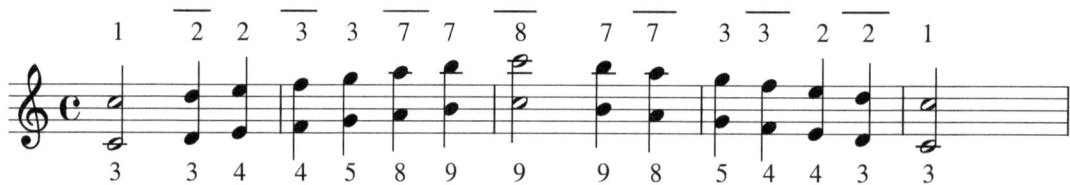

Try also exercise 1.3 from chapter 1 in octaves, as shown below:

Exercise 5.2

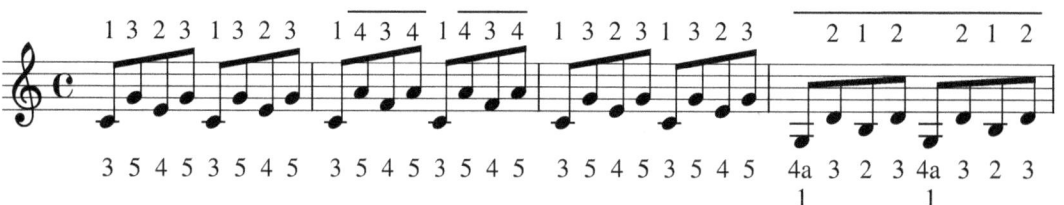

Tune 5.1

Try now 'Chamberlain Election', a tune in C which is doubled an octave below.

Chamberlain Election

Difficulty Level 4

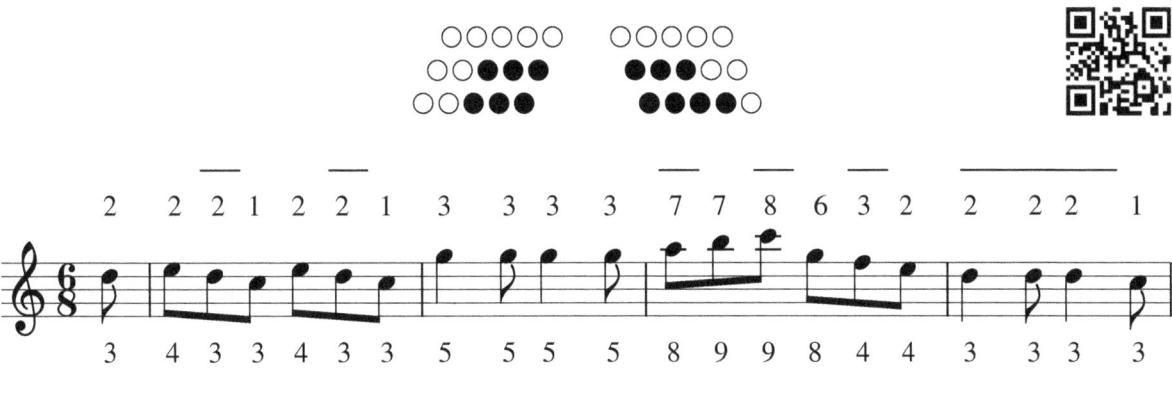

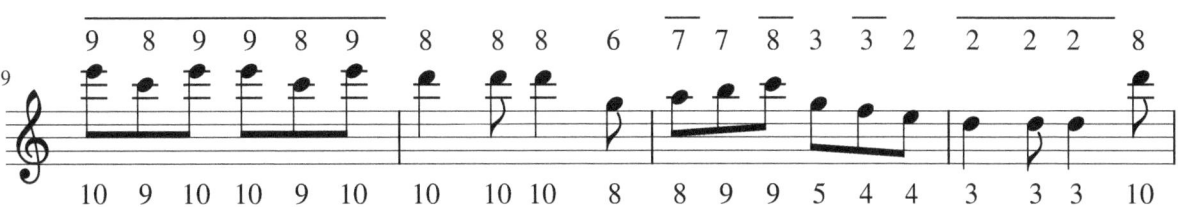

Playing in octaves in the key of G

Below is a two octave G major scale played in octaves:

Exercise 5.3

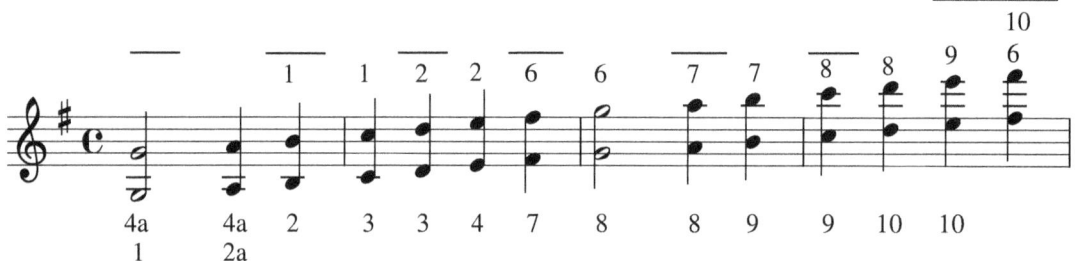

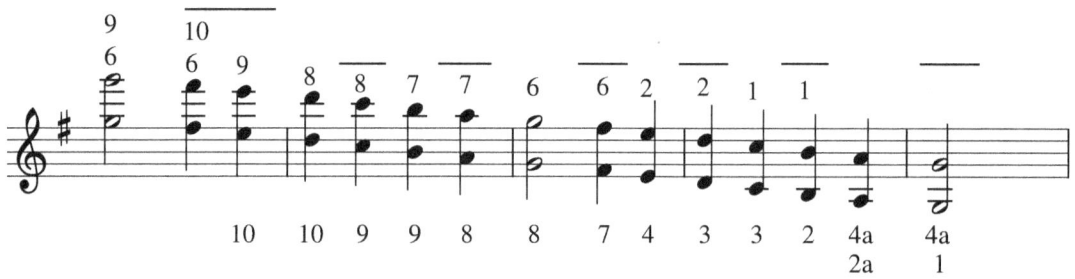

Tune 5.2

Try now 'Nineteenth of May', a tune in G in octaves, in this instance doubled an octave above written.

Nineteenth of May

Difficulty Level 4

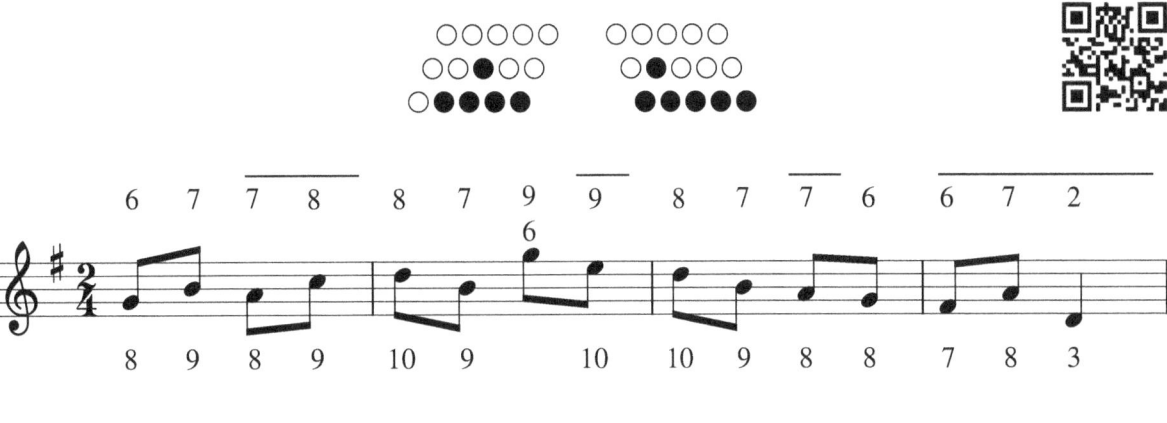

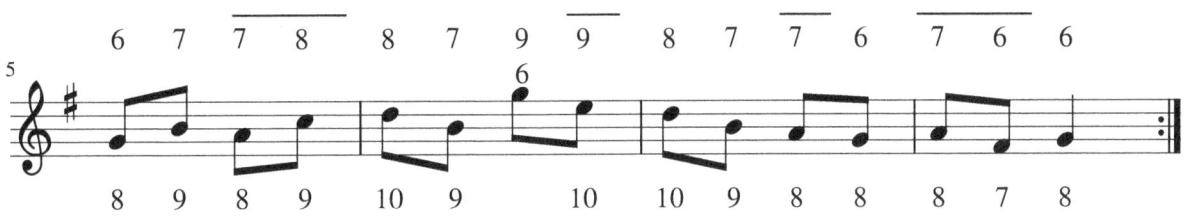

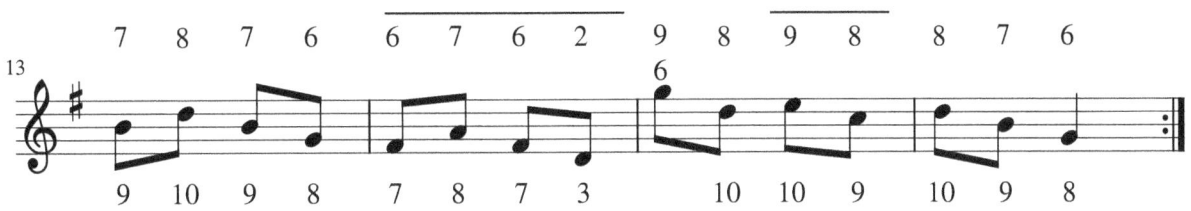

Playing in octaves in the key of D

Below is a D major scale played in octaves:

Exercise 5.4

Tune 5.3

Try now 'The London Camp' a tune in D in octaves, in this case doubled an octave lower than written.

The London Camp

Difficulty Level 4

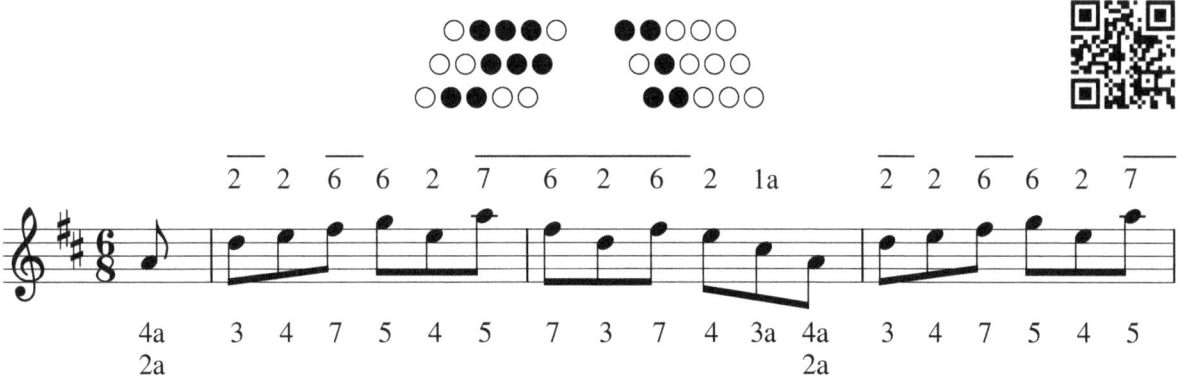

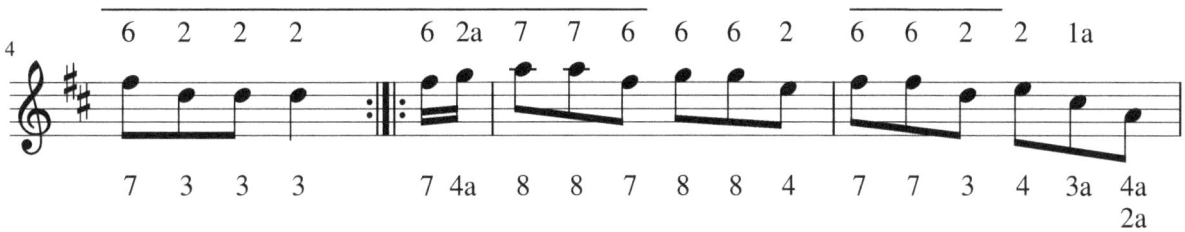

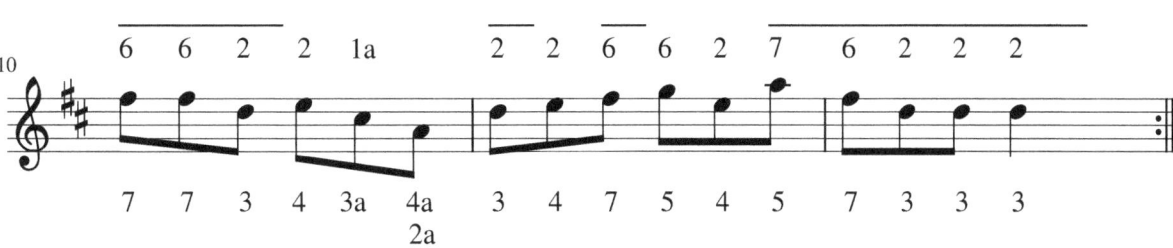

Tune 5.4

Finally, try 'Marey's Dream', a tune in the E aeolian mode, doubled an octave above the written music.

Marey's Dream

Difficulty Level 4

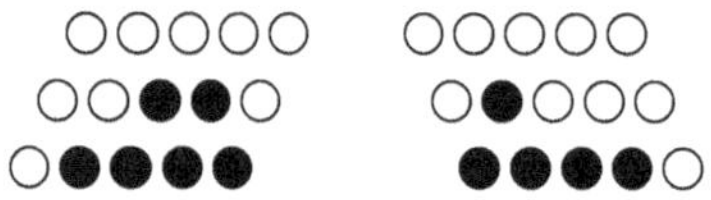

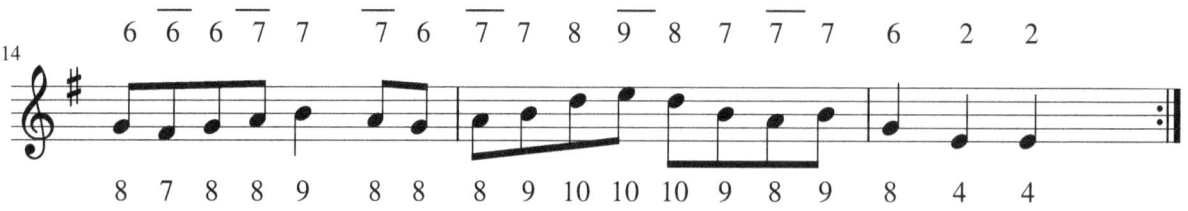

Once you can play the above tunes and exercises fluently, you will have the basic skills to play just about any tune in octaves. Now try going through the single note tunes in chapters 1 and 3 and experiment with playing them in octaves. The main consideration to make is whether to add the additional part an octave above the written tune or an octave below the written tune. This decision is made based on the range of the tune and where it fits on the concertina- as a broad rule, if the tune can mainly be played on the right hand of the concertina, the additional part should be added an octave below; if it can be mainly played on the left hand then the additional part should be added an octave above.

Chapter 6: Alternate approaches to accompaniment

In this chapter we will explore some alternate approaches to accompanying tunes, outside of the chordal vamps outlined in the previous chapters. These approaches can provide an interesting accompaniment style for tunes where chordal vamps are not appropriate or practical.

For the first tune in this chapter, Cotillon, a bass line has been added to accompany the melody. Providing a bass line as a counterpoint to a melody can be an effective way to accompany a tune in a non-chordal manner, it can also be used as a foundation for richer harmonic accompaniment as shown in the second setting of Cotillon (6.1b).

Tune 6.1a

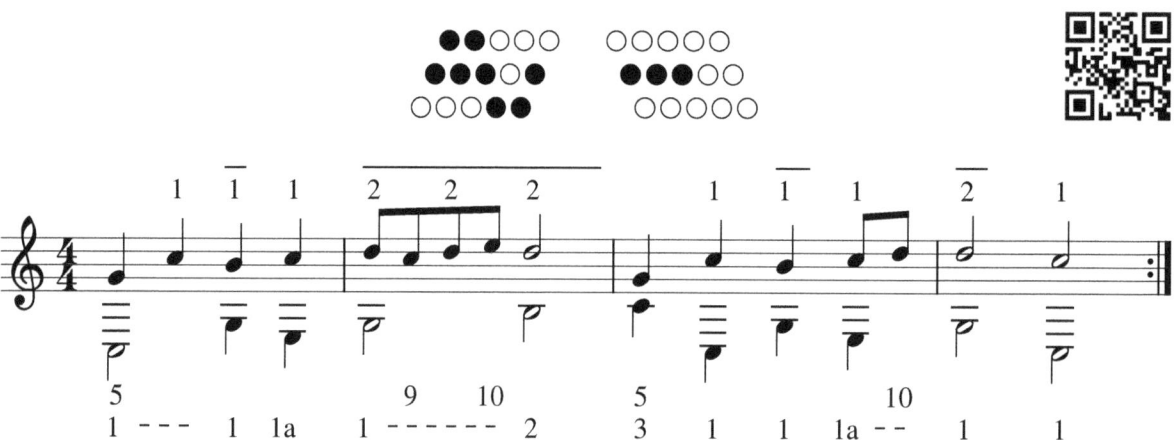

As an alternative accompaniment for Cotillon, we can take the melody and bass line from above and fill out the harmony with additional chordal notes, try tune 6.1b below for an example of how this can be done.

Tune 6.1b

Cotillon

Difficulty Level 4

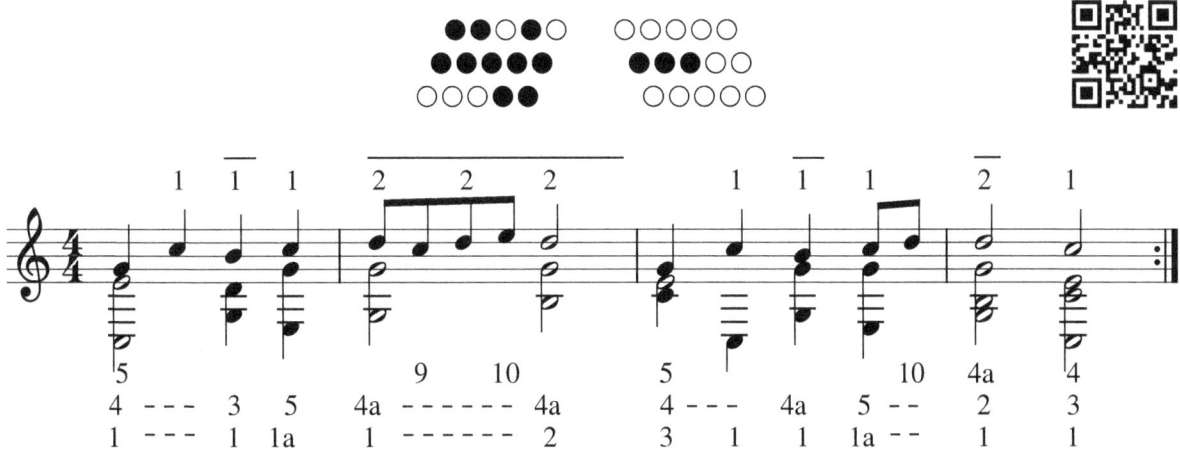

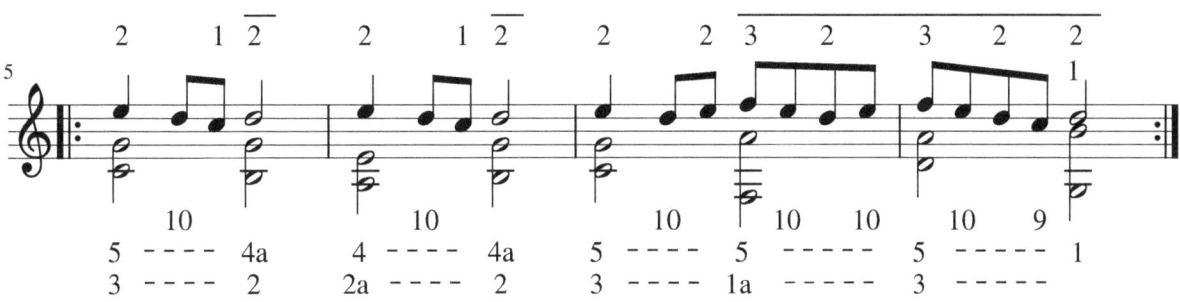

Tune 6.2

The following tune 'French March' follows a similar approach to the second setting of 'Cotillon' above, with a melody, bass line and additional chord notes to fill out the harmony.

French March

Difficulty Level 5

Anglo Concertina from Beginner to Master

In bars 9-10 and 13-14 above, the setting drops down to two voices, for these, parallel sixths and tenths are used for harmony. We have already explored parallel octaves in the previous chapters, parallel sixths and thirds (tenths above are merely thirds with an additional octave between the two notes) are common in harmony and used in a number of settings in historic concertina tutors. The following four exercises are based around playing in parallel thirds and sixths.

Exercise 6.1: A C major scale harmonised a third above

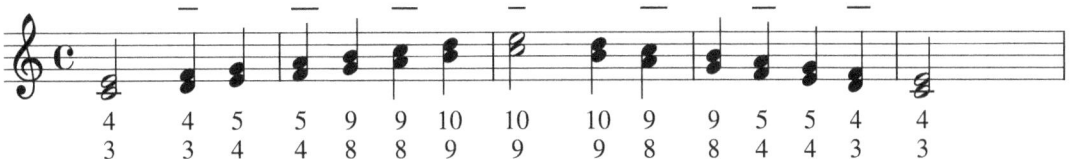

Exercise 6.2: A C major scale harmonised a third below

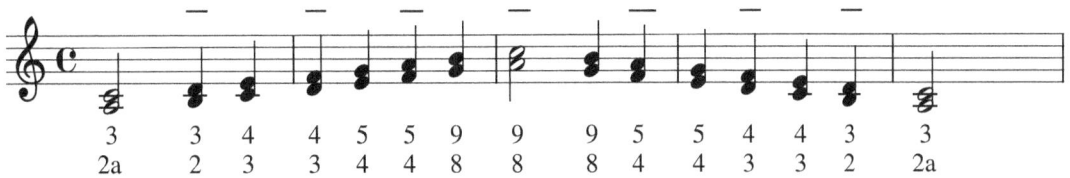

Exercise 6.3: A C major scale harmonised a sixth above

Exercise 6.4: A C major scale harmonised a sixth below

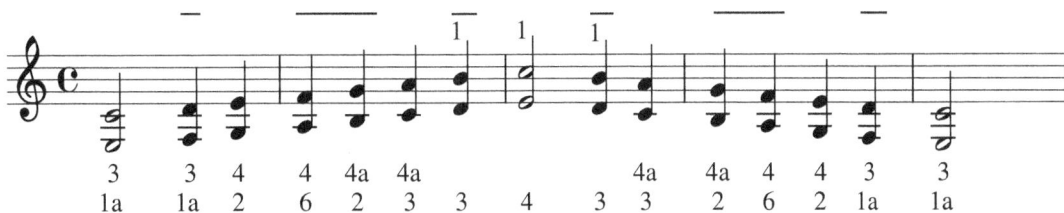

Another alternative approach to accompaniment is to provide sustained notes under the melody. For this approach, usually the root note of the chord is played beneath the tune. This is particularly effective for tunes in G or tunes that fall quite low in the concertina's range. Take for instance 'Prince William' below.

Tune 6.3

The following tune is another with just a melody and bass line. In this case, both the melody and bass line are played almost entirely on the left hand, providing a great exercise in playing two separate parts in one hand.

Tune 6.4

When once I lay with another Man's Wife

Difficulty Level 5

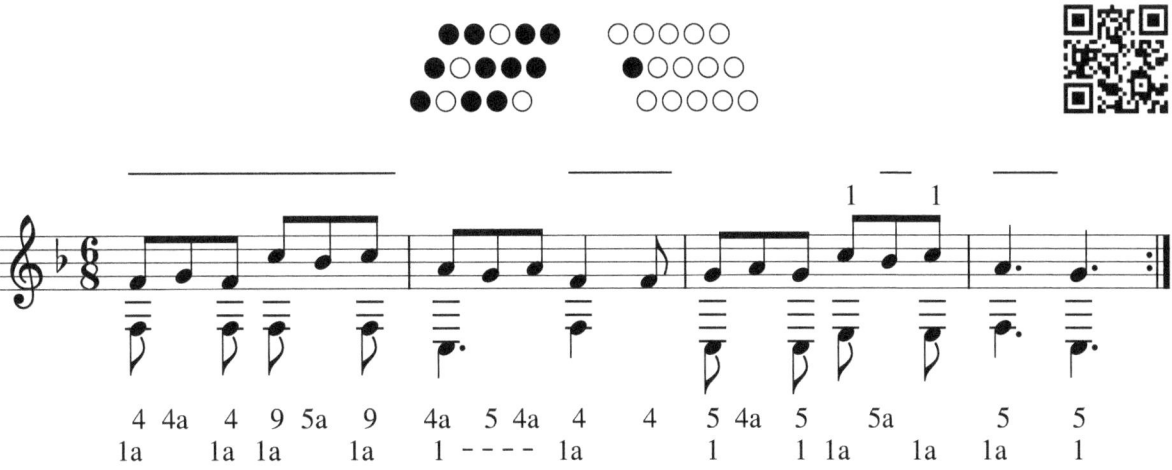

These final tunes are all based around the principal of a melody against a second counterpoint line. This is a very effective and pleasing way of playing the concertina and if you are interested in creating further settings like this, I would recommend studying classical counterpoint in more detail.

Tune 6.5

Holborn March

Difficulty Level 5

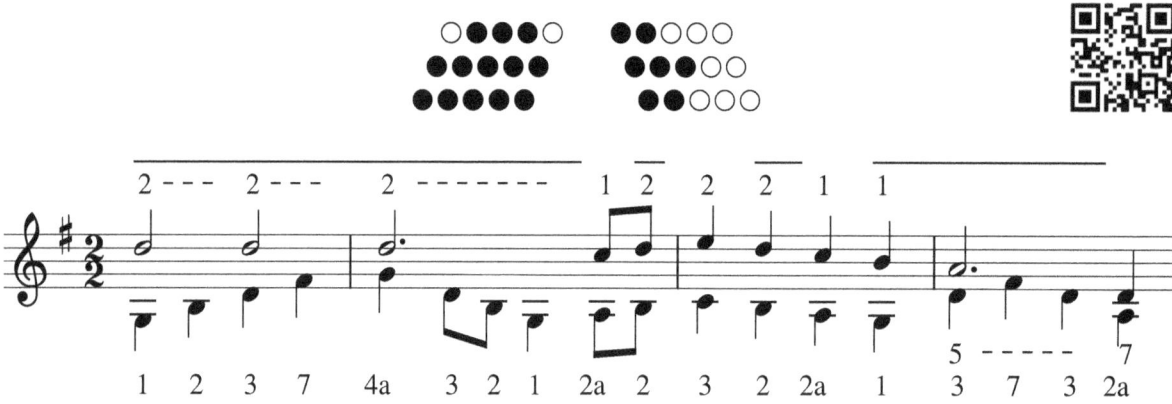

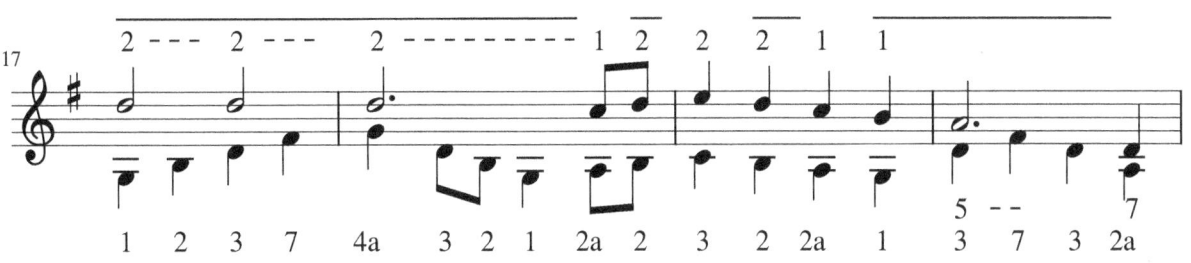

Tune 6.6

Grano's March

Difficulty Level 5

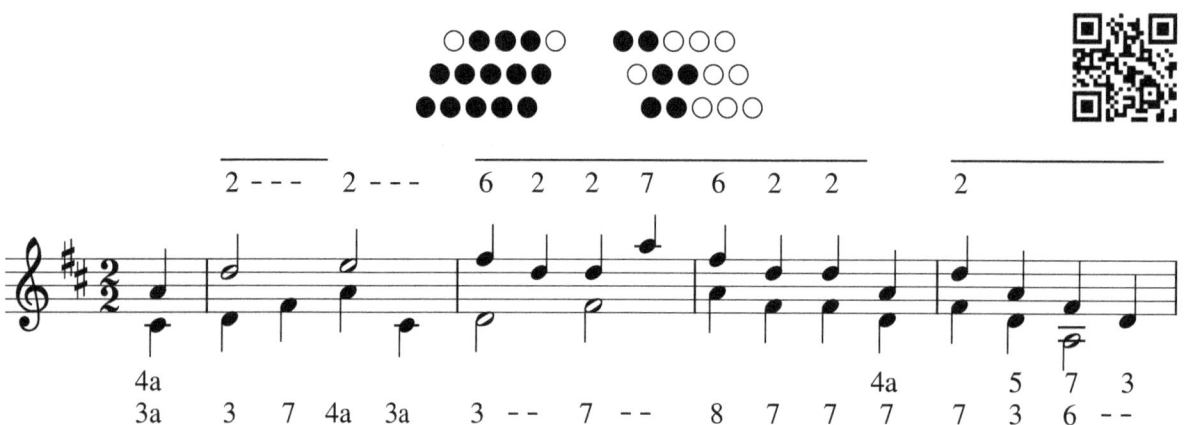

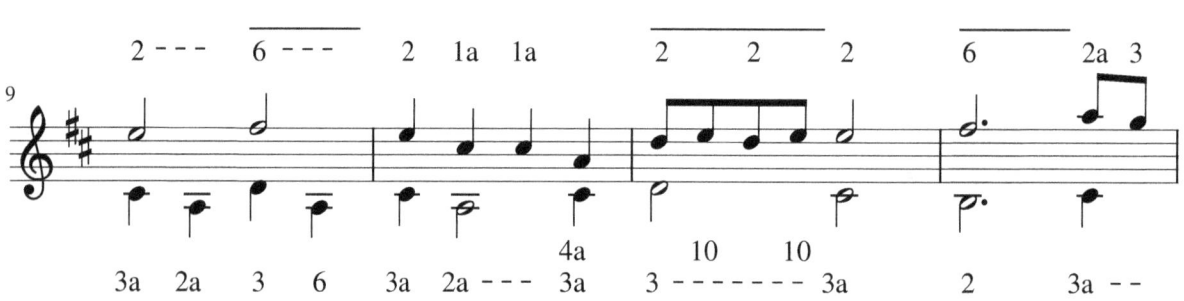

Tune 6.7

Windsor Terrace

Difficulty Level 6

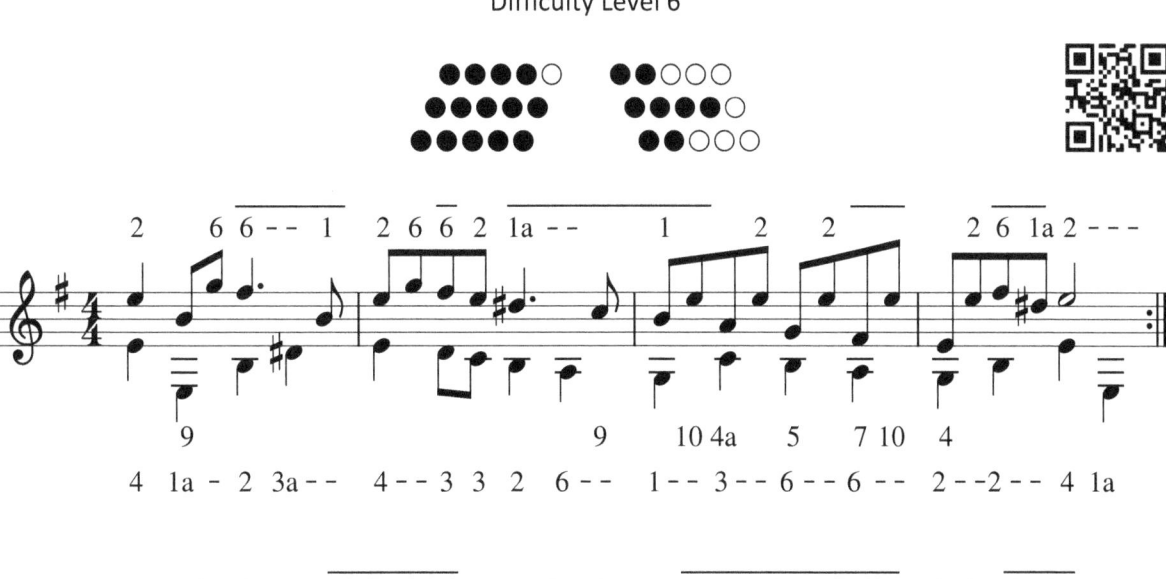
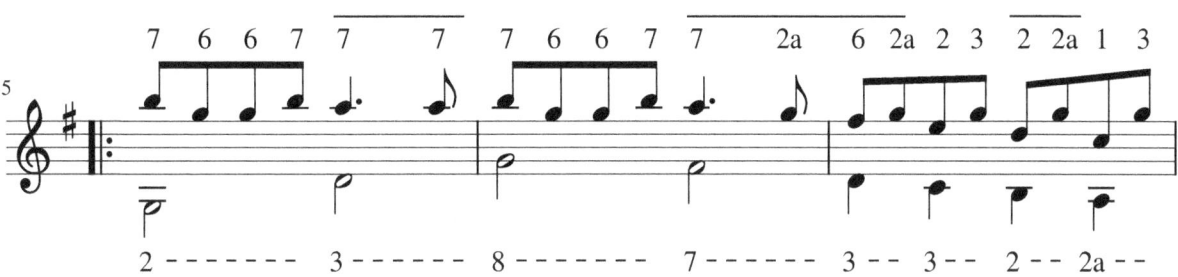
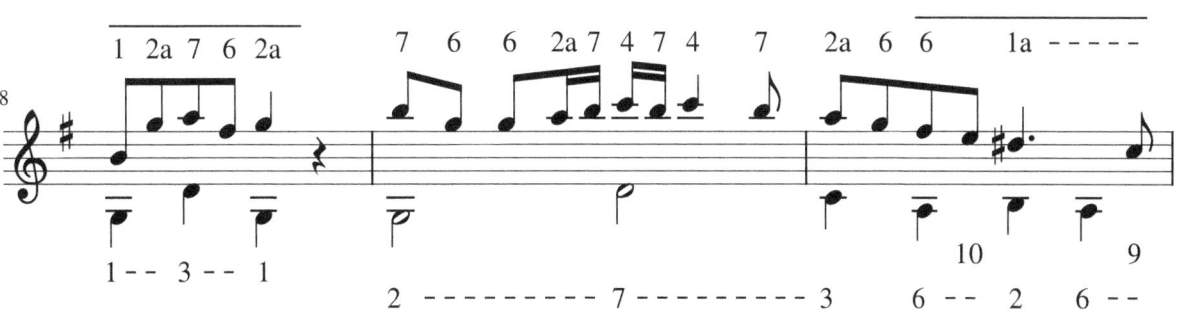
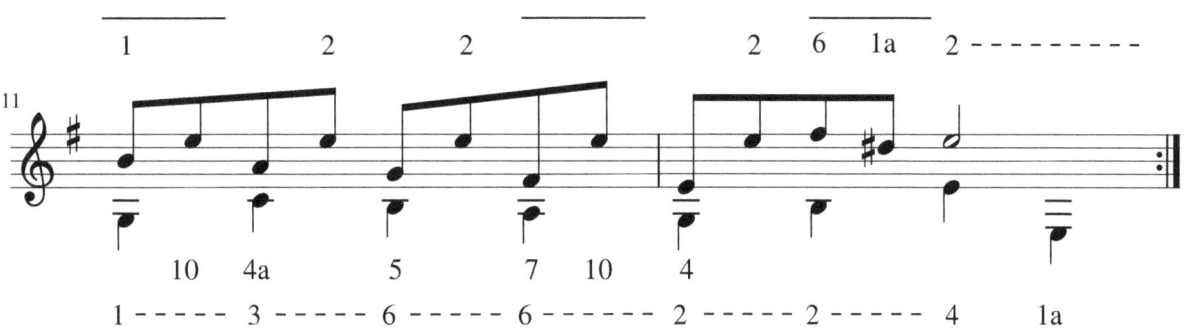

This counterpoint-based approach can be useful for accompanying tunes in more complex keys, take for example 'Maid in the Wood' below which is in G minor, accompanied using the same counterpoint accompaniment approach as above.

Tune 6.8

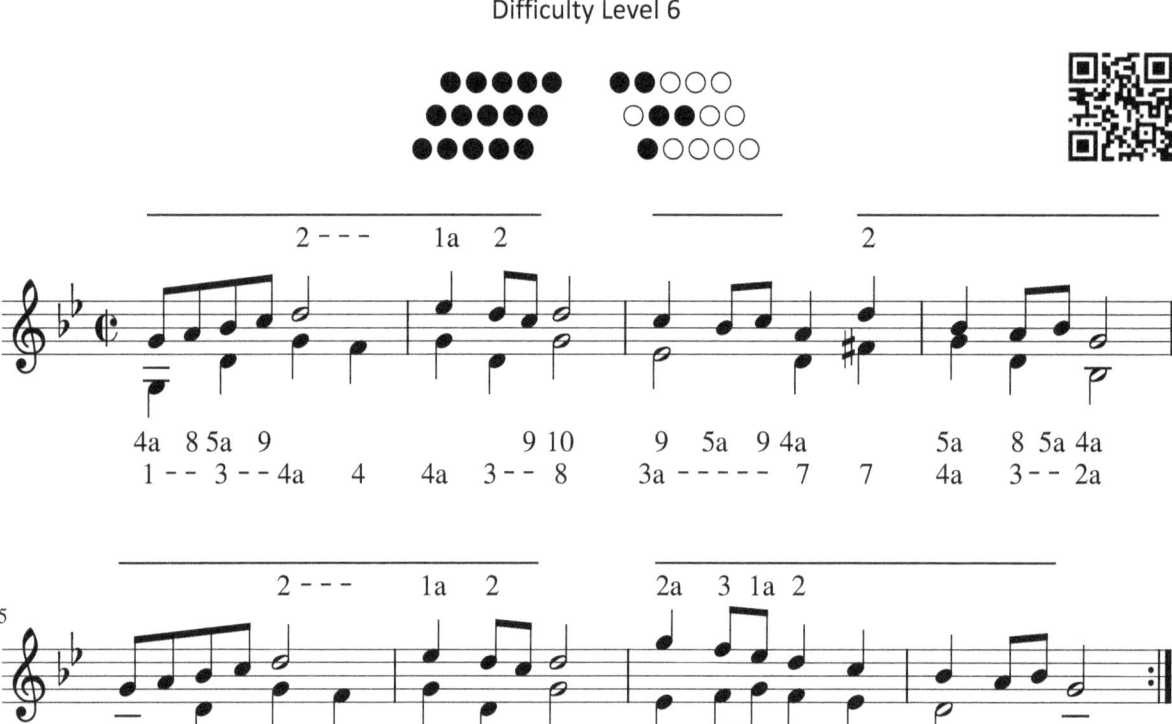

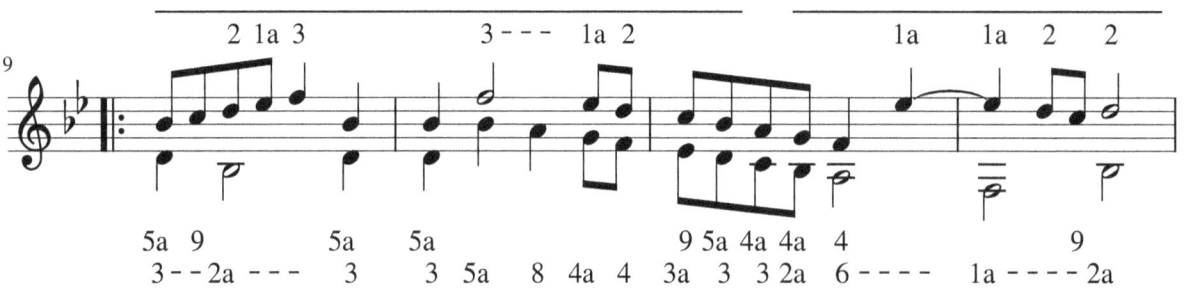
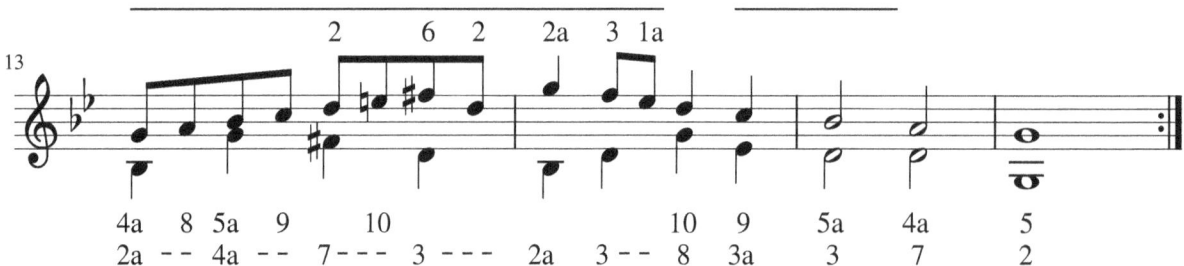

You will notice that for the tune above, there are a disproportionate number of notes on the pull of the bellows, you will need to make creative use of the air button to resolve this.

The skills and techniques covered in this chapter have numerous other musical applications. The technique of accompanying a melody using either a rhythmic or sustained bass line can be valuable for tunes low in the concertina's register, where full choral accompaniment cannot easily be achieved.

Creating the most basic bass lines in this style can be done very easily with little knowledge of music theory required; there are numerous books of tunes with guitar chords provided, simply by playing the written melody along with the root notes of the chords, you can create something in the style of the accompaniment approach demonstrated in tune 6.3, Prince William.

Through study of classical counterpoint, you can create your own harmonisations on the Anglo concertina in the style of some of the more complex setting in this chapter, which can be a very effective approach to playing tunes and to accompanying singing.

Chapter 7: Hymns

Concertinas of all systems have been long associated with the playing of hymns; concertinas were very popular with the Salvation Army for accompanying hymns, likewise almost every concertina tutorial book from the 19th century features hymn tunes in some form. Hymns are a great way to experiment with playing in a harmonic style with rich chords and independent lines.

We begin with two single note hymn tunes. These both come from Howe's *Eclectic Concertina School*. These single note tunes are a simple way to get used to the rhythms, phrasings, and melodies of hymns without needing to deal yet with complex harmonies.

Tune 7.1

Dover

Difficulty Level 1

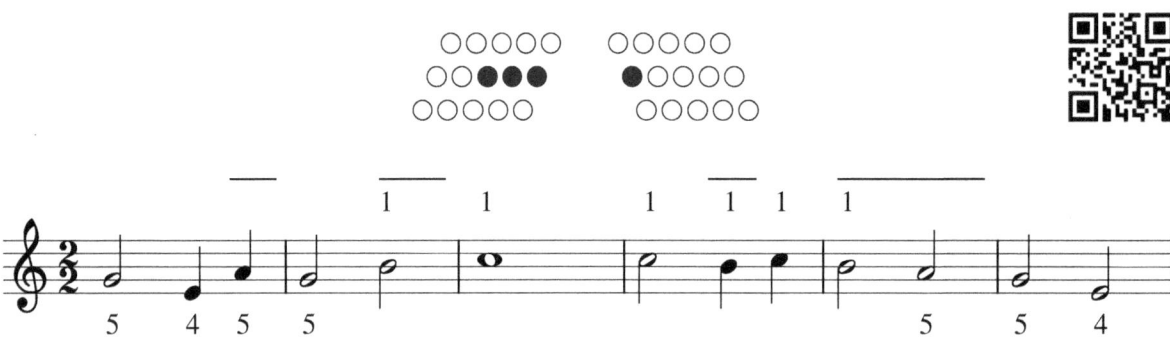

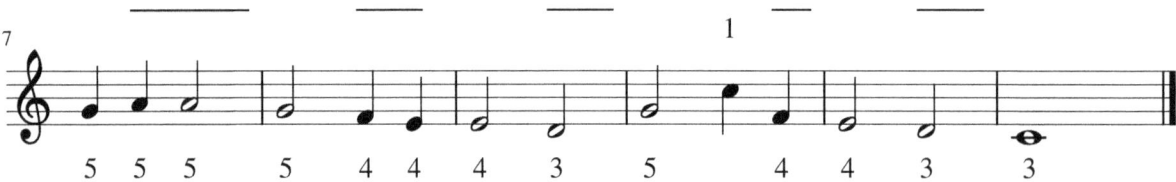

Tune 7.2

Colchester

Difficulty Level 1

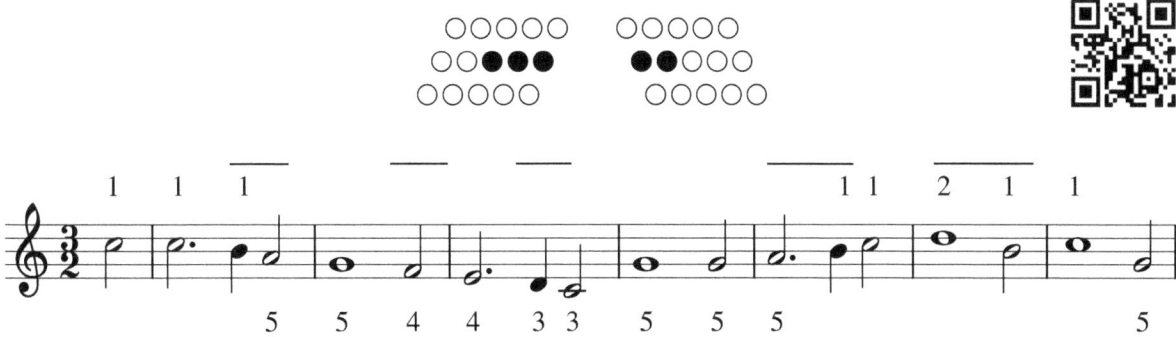

Tune 7.3, The Vespers Hymn comes from Sedgewick's *Improved Complete Instructions for German Concertina* published in 1893. It is mostly made up of two note chords and is a good introduction to harmonised hymn tunes.

Tune 7.3

The Vesper's Hymn

Difficulty Level 3

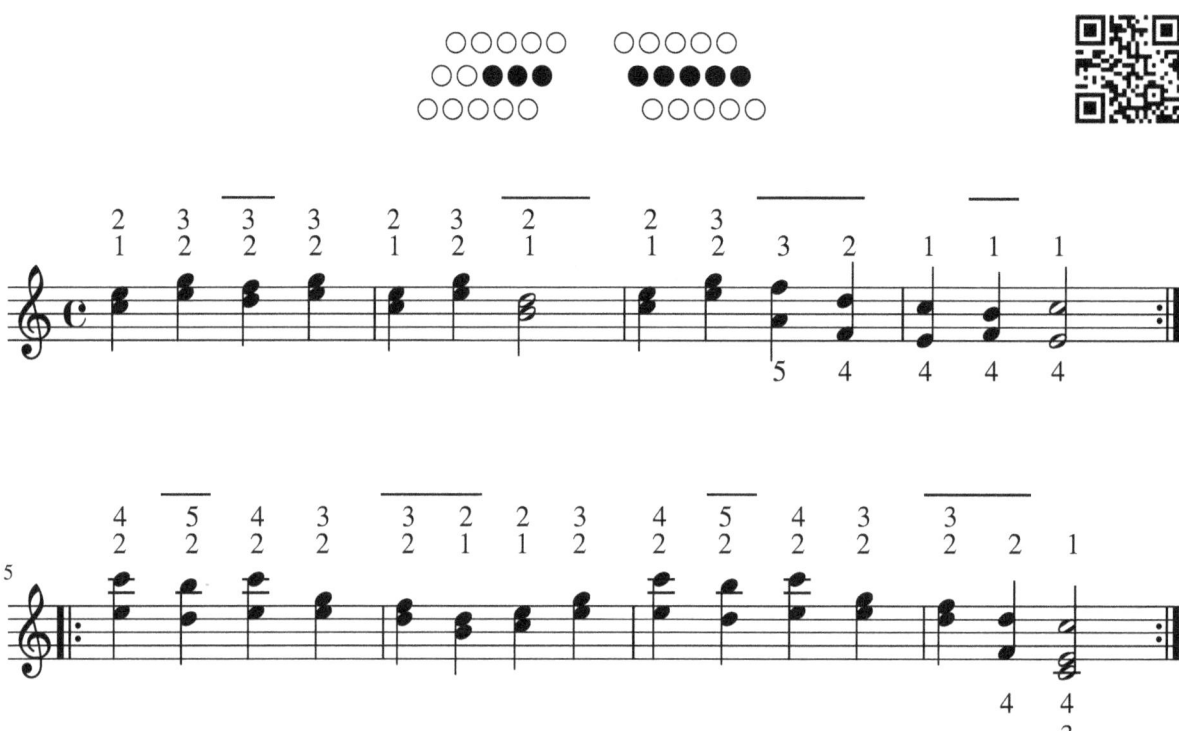

The two following tunes come from the manuscript of John Moore, a 19th century musician from Shropshire. Tune 7.4, Bridgeford, is based mainly around two note chords, while tune 7.5, Cambridge New, uses much richer four voice setting.

Tune 7.4

Bridgeford

Difficulty Level 4

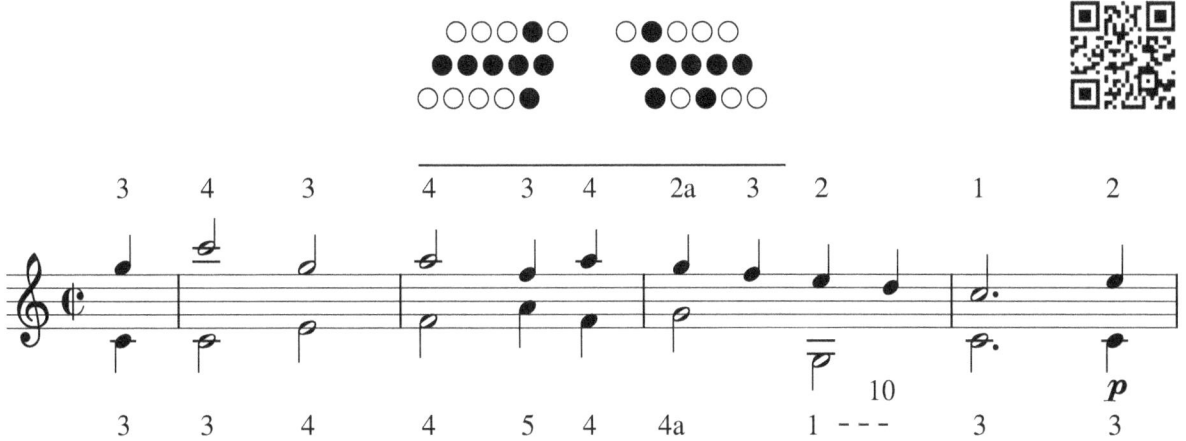
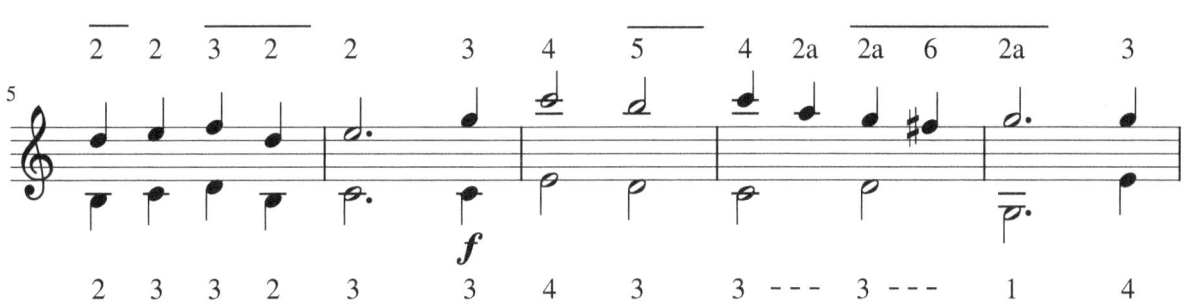
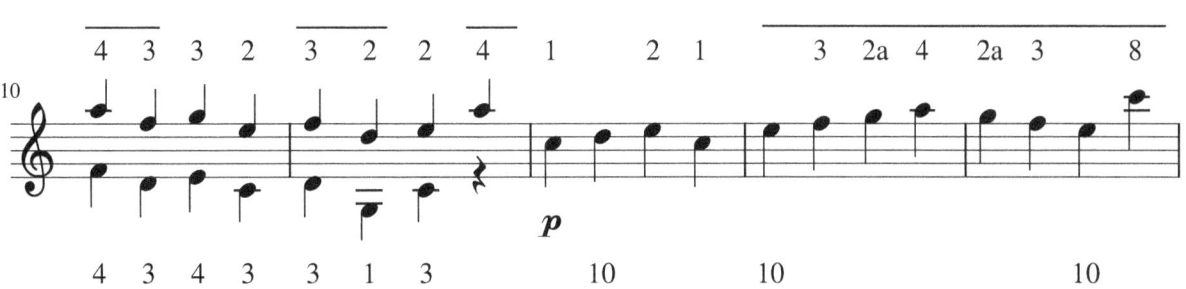
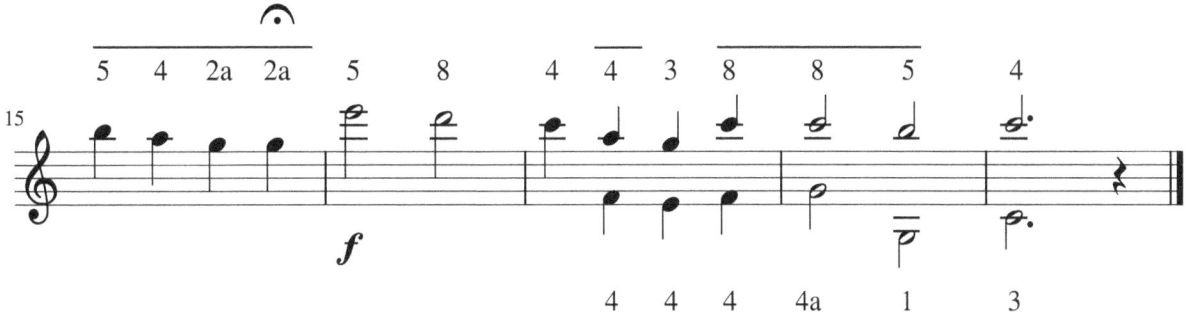

The final three tunes; Cambridge Short Tune, Oxford Tune and Martyrs Tune all come from John Playford's *Hymns and Solemn Musick.* Readers may be familiar with Playford through his *Dancing Master* series. These hymns use much more complex, richer harmonic settings, in addition, two of the three (Oxford and Martyrs) are in minor keys.

Tune 7.6

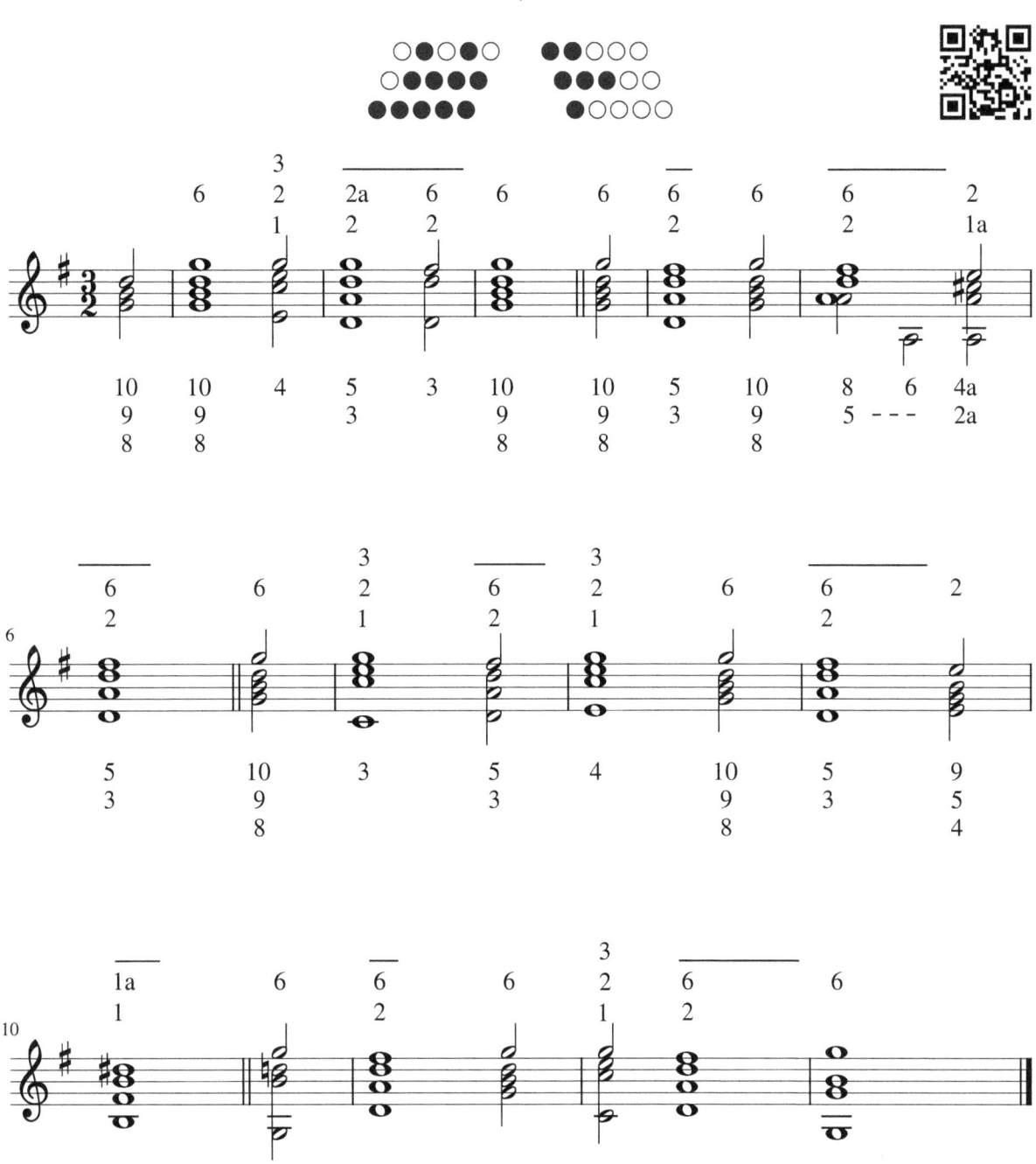

Tune 7.7

Oxford Tune

Difficulty Level 5

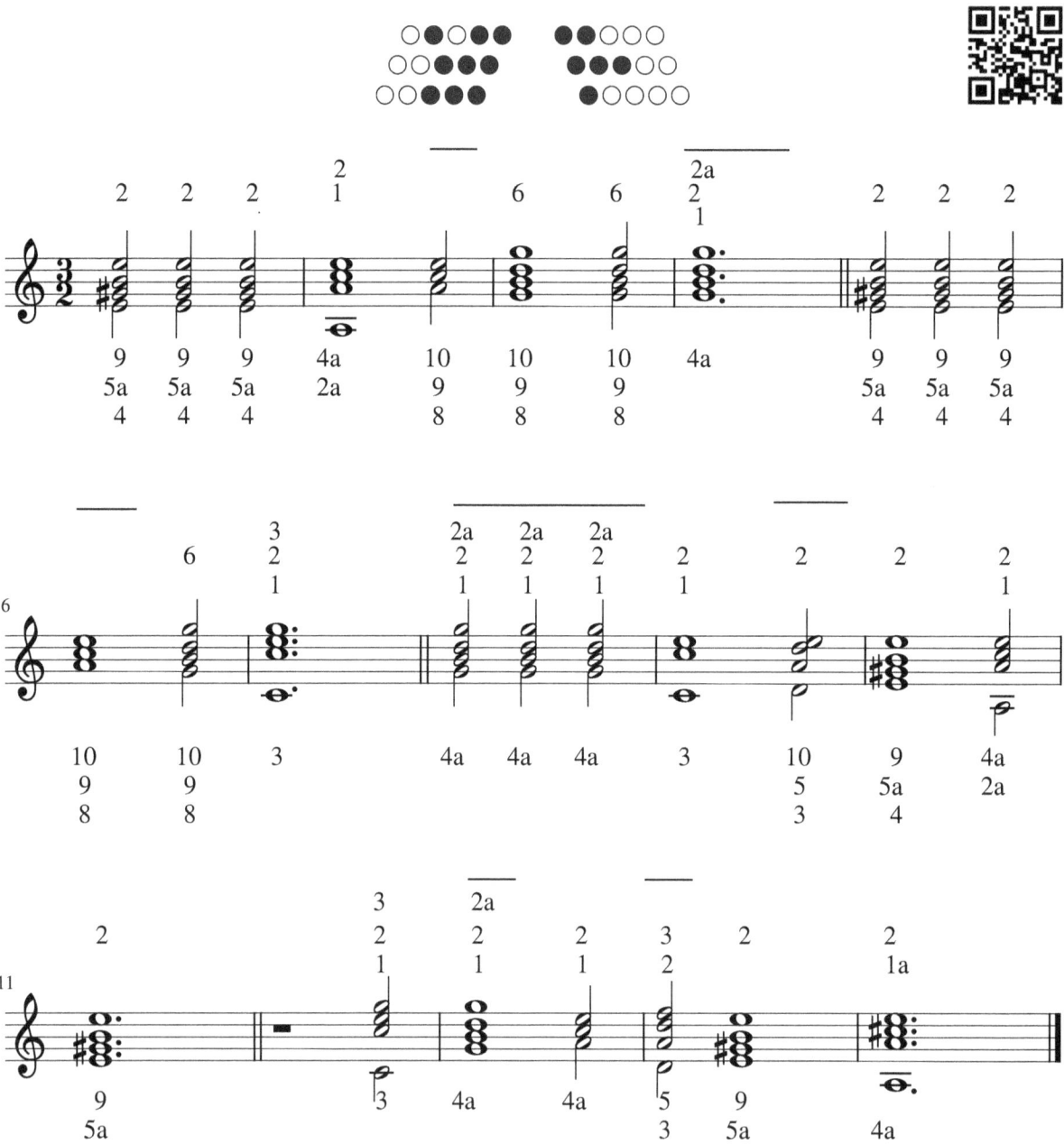

Tune 7.8

The Martyrs Tune

Difficulty Level 5

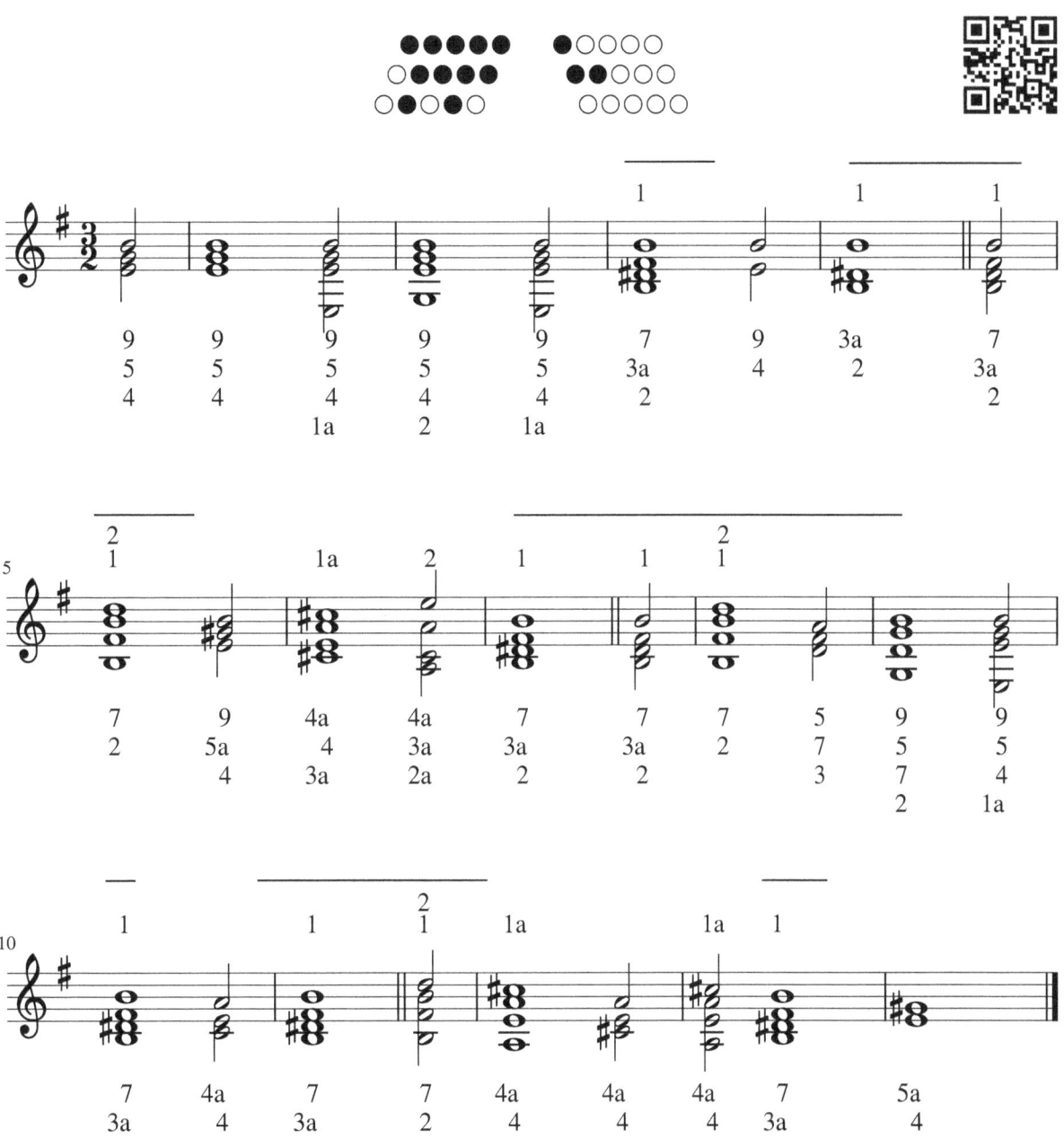

Concluding remarks

The above is just a brief introduction into hymns arranged for the concertina. There are a huge number of hymns available, readily harmonised, which can be played on the concertina with little or no adaptation and are a great way to explore rich harmonic playing. In addition to the sources cited above, I would recommend *Hymns Ancient and Modern* and *The English Hymnal* as excellent resources for harmonised hymn tunes.

Chapter 8: Baroque

One of my greatest interests as a concertina player is the exploration of music of the Baroque era, and I have chosen to dedicate the final chapter of this book to that. It is surprising how much music by Baroque masters such as Bach, Handel, Purcell and many others can fit readily on the Anglo (sometimes with a little gentle encouragement) and be effectively performed on the instrument.

This final chapter presents two multi-movement pieces by two Baroque composers. The first piece is Georg Philipp Telemann's 5th Fantasia for solo flute, and the second is Johann Paul von Westhoff's 4th Partita for solo violin. Although they are both challenging pieces, they draw heavily on ideas that we have discussed in previous chapters.

With both pieces, the music for each movement is presented in full first, followed by advice for technique and interpretation on the Anglo concertina. In neither case should my suggestions be seen as the definitive approach to performing these pieces on the Anglo concertina; I would recommend listening to some of the numerous recordings that have been made of these pieces to hear how players have interpreted these pieces on the instruments for which they were intended.

Telemann's 5th Fantasia for solo flute

This is the fifth of twelve fantasias for solo flute written by Telemann in around 1732. Since the piece was written for flute, it is entirely a single line with no chords. Nevertheless, the piece draws heavily on 'implied polyphony', so although only a single line is sounding, conceptually there are multiple voices active at any one time.

First Movement

Difficulty Level 5

Telemann

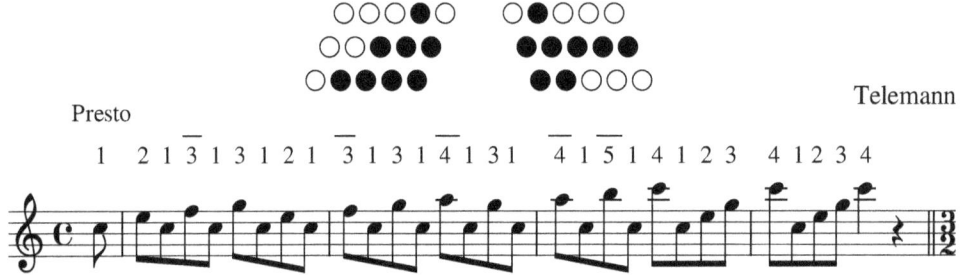

This movement should be thought of as a prelude to the fantasia, it is based around the juxtaposition between slow and fast sections. The fast sections are marked as presto (try around minim=100) the slow sections are marked as largo and dolce, despite the use of two different terms they should both be played at around the same speed (try around minim=80); for reference, largo means slow while dolce means gentle and sweet.

Ornamentation

In the case of this movement, some ornamentation is indicated, trills are indicated in this piece in bars 8 and 16. Additionally grace notes are also indicated in bars 5, 6, 7, 13, 14 and 15.

There are some possibilities to add additional ornaments, for instance the arpeggio in bar 4 can be filled with an ascending scale as shown in the example 8.1 below:

Example 8.1: ornamentation for bar 4.

Likewise an F# grace note can be added before the final g in bar 12 as shown in the example 8.2 below:

Example 8.2: ornamentation for bar 12.

Second Movement

Difficulty Level 7

Telemann

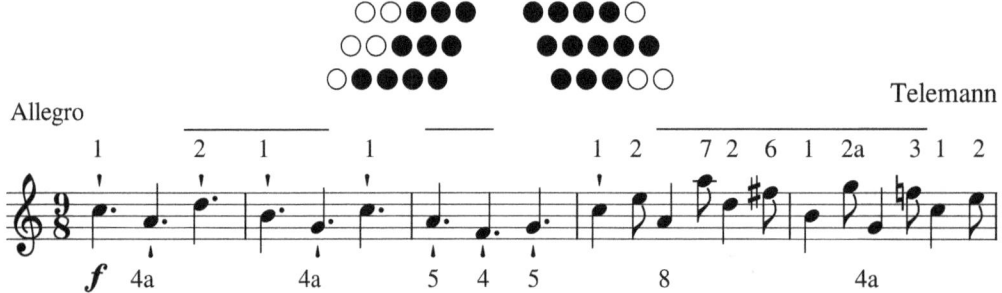

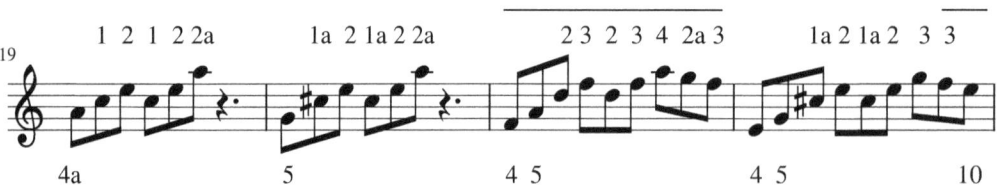
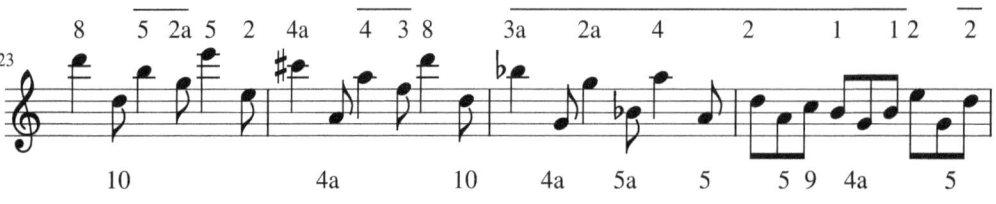

This second movement is a passacaglia based around a series of variations of a harmonic structure laid out in the first three bars. This movement draws heavily on implied polyphony and an important consideration with this movement is to bring out the dialogue between the voices. The movement is usually played at a tempo of around dotted crochet=90.

The movement begins with the main subject in bars 1-3, to emphasise this subject, play with a clear tone, with the forte (loud) dynamics indicated on the score. It is worth noting that in the following bars (4-9) the subject appears twice more as two other implied voices are added.

Example 8.3: The appearances of the subject in bars 1-9.

The above example shows the way in which the subject is repeated in bars 4-9 with the addition of further voices. Notice that the notes marked with an asterisk (*) in bars 4-9 are the same as the notes of the subject in bars 1-3. To bring out the repetition of the subject as additional voices are added, use louder dynamics on the notes marked with asterisks above.

The subject from bars 1-3 appears again in bars 42-47 and 51-53. As before, bring out the notes of the subject at this point using dynamic contrast.

Example 8.4: The appearances of the subject in bars 42-47.

Example 8.5: The appearance of the subject in bars 51-54.

The above bars 51-54 also provide a resolution for the open subject. Notice that the tonic (C) is stated in the final bar in the outer voice (marked O) and the inner voice (marked I). Even where the subject is not present, there is clear dialogue between the voices which can be brought out using dynamics. For this movement, I recommend that you keep a simple sound with little ornamentation to keep the clarity in voices.

You will notice that the sharp signs in bar 35 are in brackets- these are editorial accidentals that I have added, these do not appear in Teleman's manuscript nor in many *urtext* editions of this piece, they are however as most players choose to interpret this bar.

Third Movement

Difficulty Level 5

This final movement is an allegro in the style of a gigue. Many flautists tend to perform this at a slightly slower tempo than a standard gigue, generally around dotted crochet=80.

This movement allows for greater opportunity to explore ornamentation, besides the trills shown in bars 19 and 20, there are numerous other possible ornaments, below are a few examples.

Example ornaments:

Bars 10-12. The leap of a sixth in bar 10 can be filled in with an ascending scale, trills can be used at the start of bars 11 and 12 and a grace note can be used before the high A in bar 12.

Example 8.6: Ornamentation for bars 10-12.

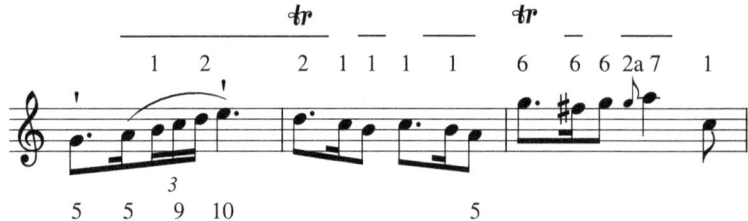

Bars 27-28. Grace notes can be used in bars 27 and 28 before the high C and D respectively.

Example 8.7: Ornamentation for bars 27-28.

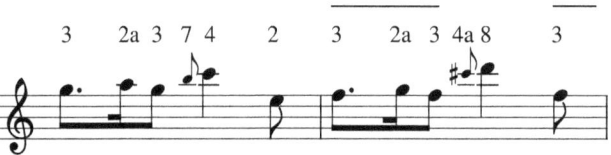

Bars 32-36. The leap of a sixth in bar 32 can be filled in with an ascending scale, a trill can be used at the start of bar 33 and grace notes can be used at various points in bars 34, 35 and 36.

Example 8.8: Ornamentation for bars 32-36.

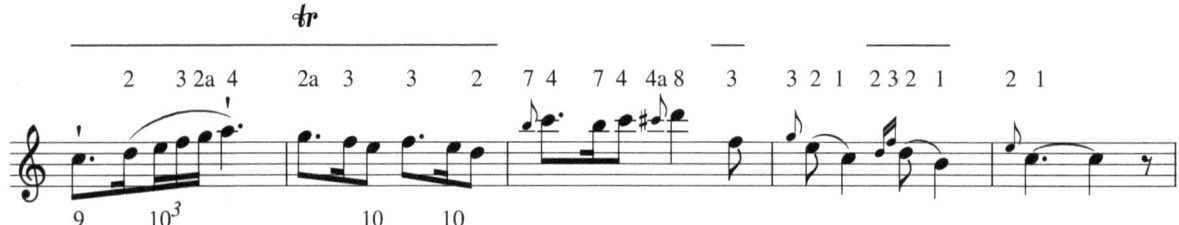

Because each section repeats, perhaps experiment with ornamentation on the repeats, i.e. for the first iteration of a section play it as written, then add ornamentation for the repeats.

Westhoff's 4th Partita for solo violin

This work is the fourth of six partitas (dance suites) for solo violin composed by Johann Paul von Westhoff in the late 17th century. The piece follows the standard form of a dance suite, beginning with an allemande, followed by a courante then a sarabande and finally a gigue.

The piece is an exploration of the polyphonic capabilities of the unaccompanied violin and thus draws heavily on multiple stopped chords. In some cases, compromises may need to be made to the written music, in particular, concertina players will need to break or shorten some of the written chords.

All of these movements feature sections which repeat, providing opportunities to alter articulation and ornamentation on repeats.

The four movements are presented in the order in which they would be performed, however they do not appear in the order of easiest to most complex, thus I recommend learning the sarabande first, followed by the courante, then the allemande and finally the gigue.

Westhoff 4th Partita for Solo Violin:

Allemande

Difficulty Level 7

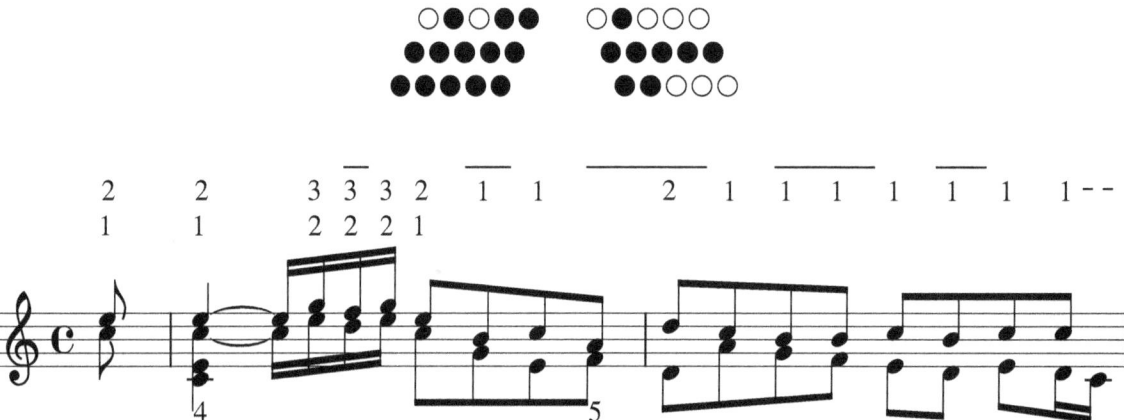

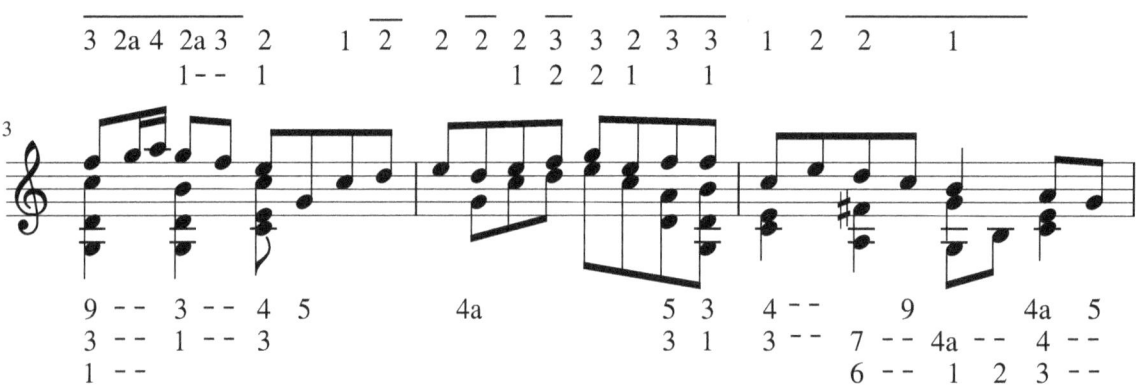

This first movement is an Allemande, a slow dance, for this movement I suggest a tempo of around crochet=55. I would recommend trying to achieve a smooth, lyrical quality to your performance of this movement.

Note that in bar 10, the written music and the tablature do not match up- this is because the written music preserves the original indications from the composer whereas the tablature has been adapted to fit a standard 30 key Anglo concertina. In this bar, the composer includes a low G sharp, however many Anglo concertinas do not have this note, if you do have this note, I would recommend including it as indicated through the written music, if you do not have it, follow the tablature. For reference, the tablature for this bar if expressed in written music would be as below.

In bar 15, you will notice that the sharp sign before the first F has been added editorially, again, this does not appear in the written source for this piece, however it is how most performer choose to interpret this bar.

Courante

Difficulty Level 7

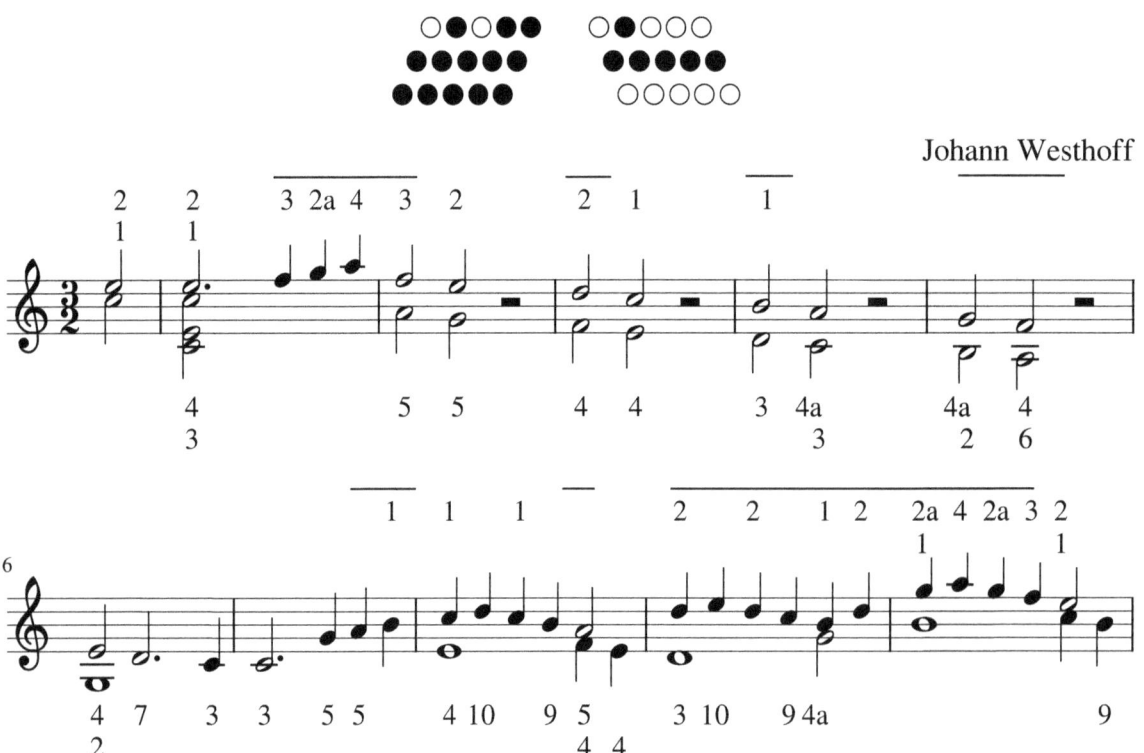

Johann Westhoff

A courante is an energetic dance in triple time. For this movement, I would recommend a tempo of around minim=185. Try using snappy, staccato articulation to bring out the lively character of this movement, try to make the notes in bars 2-5 particularly crisp to bring out the rests at the end of those bars. Experiment also with ornamentation, I would recommend in particular trying to incorporate trill on the B in bar 21 and the first B in bar 28.

Anglo Concertina from Beginner to Master

Sarabande

Difficulty Level 5

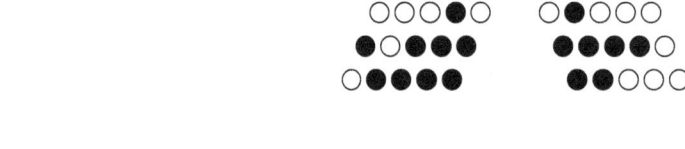

A sarabande is a slow dance in triple time. For this movement, I would recommend a tempo of around minim=65. Aim for smooth bellows changes and button articulations to bring out the lyrical quality of this movement. This is also an ideal piece to experiment with incorporating ornaments, try for instance placing trills on the first F sharp in bar 10, the F sharp in bar 14 and the B in bar 18.

This is a good example of a piece where large blocks of music can be played in a few different positions and using different bellows directions across the keyboard. Experiment with using different fingerings for sections of this tune and consider incorporating these as variations on repeats.

Gigue

Difficulty Level 7

Johann Westhoff

A gigue is a lively dance, closely related to the jig. This gigue is undoubtedly the most complex piece in this book and will probably take some work to execute on a 30 key Anglo concertina. I would recommend a target tempo of around dotted semibreve=80. As with the courante, aim for a strong and snappy tone and articulation to bring out the energy of this movement. Some simple ornamentation can be effective, however, due to the energy and contrapuntal complexity of this movement, I would recommend avoiding over embellishing the movement.

Sources

Chapter 1:

1.1 Waltz: Elias Howe, *Howe's Western German Concertina School* (Boston: Elias Howe, 1879)

1.2 Such a Wife as Willy Had: William Vickers manuscript, c. 1770

1.3 Bryan O'Lynn: Elias Howe, *Howe's Eclectic School For the Concertina* (Boston: Elias Howe, 1879)

1.4 The Christmas Tale: Charles & Samuel Thompson, *Twenty four Country Dances for the year 1778* (London: Thompson, 1778)

1.5 The Magic Girdle: William Randall, *Twenty Four Country Dances for the Year 1771* (London: Randall, 1771)

1.6 The Devil in a Bush: Vickers MS

1.7 West Cottage Hornpipe: Albert John Hughes manuscript, 19th century

1.8 Rattling Morgan: Mr Gray, *Twenty Four Country Dances for the Year 1803* (London: Thompson, 1803)

1.9 The Tempest: N. Stewart, *A Select Collection of Scots English Irish and Foreign Airs, Jiggs & Marches* (Edinburgh: Stewart, 1784)

1.10 All Around the Maypole See How They Trot: John Clare manuscript, c. 1820-1834

1.11 Marybone Assembly: John Walsh, *Country Dances Selected, Part 1* (London: Walsh, n.d.)

1.12 Fishes in the Sea: Alfred B. Sedgwick, *Sedgwick's Improved and Complete Instructions for the German Concertina* (Boston: Oliver Ditson & co., 1865)

1.13 Favourite Banjo Breakdown: Charles Roylance, *The Anglo German Concertina Players Companion* (London: Roylance, 1889)

1.14 Sailor's Hornpipe: Roylance, *The Anglo German Concertina Players Companion*

1.15 Cat's Polka: Frank Kidson and Alfred Moffat, *100 Singing Games* (Glasgow: Bayley & Ferguson, 1916)

1.16 Beautiful Star: Sedgwick, *Improved and Complete Instructions*

Chapter 2:

2.1 Minasi Number 3: Carlo Minasi, *Instruction book for the German Concertina* (London: Kleyser & Tritschler, 1846)

2.2 Minasi Number 7: Minasi, *Instruction book for the German Concertina*

2.3 Waltz: *Howe's Western German Concertina School*

2.4 Tyroler Waltzer: Johann Gottlieb Höselbarth, *Anweisung das Accordion zu spielen* (Chemnitz: Höselbarth, c. 1837)

2.5 Westwood Park: Joshua Jackson manuscript, 1798

2.6 Lichfield Races: Vickers MS

2.7 Lady Cathcart: Thomas Preston, *Twenty Four Country Dances for the year 1801* (London: Preston, 1801)

2.8 The Exile: Button & Whitakers, *Dances, Reels and Waltzes, no. 11* (London: Button & Whitakers, c. 1815)

2.9 The Birmingham March: John Moore manuscript, book 2, 19th century

2.10 Labarynth: Betham manuscript, c. 1815

2.11 Tekeli: Betham MS

2.12 Honey Moon: Betham MS

2.13 Paddy Wack: Joseph Barnes manuscript, .c 1762-69

2.14 Frogmore Farm: Thomas Sands manuscript, 1810

2.15 Miss Gayton's Hornpipe: John Baty manuscript, c. 1850-60

Chapter 3:

3.1 Ellingham Assembly: Vickers MS

3.2 Now or Never: Vickers MS

3.3 King's Polka: Henry Stables manuscript, 19th century

3.4 The Philosopher's Jigg: Longman, Twenty Four Country Dances for the Year 1770 (London: Longman, 1770)

3.5 Trip to London: George Spencer manuscript, 1831

3.6 Saxon Hornpipe: Moore MS, book 2

3.7 Take a Dance: David Rutherford, *Rutherford's Compleat Collection of 200 of the most celebrated Country Dances, Vol 2* (London: Rutherford, c. 1759)

3.8 The Unfortunate Cup of Tea: Elias Howe, *Musician's Omnibus, No. 2* (Boston: Elias Howe, [c. 1863])

3.9 Wilkes's Wriggle: Robert Harrison manuscript, c. 1815

3.10 The Fiddler's Jig: Vickers MS

3.11 Welsh Fusileer: David Young manuscript

3.12 Cure For All Grief: Frank Kidson, *Old English Country Dances* (London: William Reeves, 1890)

3.13 Harliquin Air: Benjamin Cooke manuscript, c. 1770

3.14 Two and Two: Kidson, *Old English Country Dances*

Chapter 4:

4.1 Union Waltz: Elias Howe, *First Part of the Musical Companion* (Boston: Oliver Ditson, [c. 1842])

4.2 Buds of May: William Cahusac, *Twenty Four Country Dances for the year 1809* (London: Cahusac, 1809)

4.3 Spring's Waltz: Elias Howe, *Musician's Omnibus, No. 6* (Boston: Elias Howe, [c. 1863])

4.5 Freedom and Liberty: James Blackshaw manuscript, 1837

4.6 Rakish Highlandman: Thomas Wilson, *A Companion to the Ballroom* (London: D MacKay, [c. 1816])

Chapter 5:

Tune 5.1 Chamberlain Election: Anonymous manuscript in the Vaughan Williams Memorial Library

Tune 5.2 Nineteenth of May: Walsh, *Country Dances Selected, Part 1*

Tune 5.3 The London Camp: Stewart, *A Select Collection*

Tune 5.4 Marey's Dream: John Miller manuscript, 1799

Chapter 6:

6.1 Cotillon: John Gay, *The Beggar's Opera* (London: John Watts, 1728)

6.2 French March: Henry Atkinson manuscript, 1694

6.3 Prince William: John Johnson, *Choice Collection of Favourite Country Dances, Volume* 1 (London: Johnson [c. 1750])

6.4 When once I lay with another Man's Wife: Gay, *The Beggar's Opera*

6.5 Holborn March: Johnson, *Choice Collection vol 1*

6.6 Grano's March: Johnson, *Choice Collection vol 1*

6.7 Windsor Terrace: Kidson, *Old English Country Dances*

6.8 Maid in the Wood: John Johnson, *Choice Collection of Favourite Country Dances, Volume* 2 (London: Johnson [c. 1750])

Chapter 7:

7.1 Dover: *Howe's Eclectic School for the Concertina*

7.2 Colchester: *Howe's Eclectic School for the Concertina*

7.3 The Vesper's Hymn: Sedgwick, *Improved and Complete Instructions*

7.4 Bridgeford: Moore MS, book 3

7.5 Cambridge New: Moore MS, book 3

7.6 Cambridge Short Tune: John Playford, *Psalms & Hymns in Solemn Musick* (London: Playford, 1671)

7.7 Oxford Tune: Playford, *Psalms & Hymns in Solemn Musick*

7.8 The Martyrs Tune: Playford, *Psalms & Hymns in Solemn Musick*

Chapter 8:

Telemann Flute Fantasia 5: First Edition, published c. 1732

Westhoff Violin Partita 4: First Edition, published 1696

Video Links

Chapter 1

Tune 1.1 Waltz: https://youtu.be/ZyMmVMQTojI

Tune 1.2 Such a Wife as Willy Had: https://youtu.be/X5NMrceLl88

Tune 1.3 Bryan O'Lynn: https://youtu.be/aaxim9GR7vs

Tune 1.4 The Christmas Tale: https://youtu.be/yokXnRcE890

Tune 1.5 The Magic Girdle: https://youtu.be/trVqPI_1oaM

Tune 1.6 The Devil in a Bush: https://youtu.be/cM-KiGmpuxM

Tune 1.7 West Cottage Hornpipe: https://youtu.be/_lOPA4uXuFw

Tune 1.8 Rattling Morgan: https://youtu.be/WgwuCw7JoLA

Tune 1.9 The Tempest: https://youtu.be/4rgZvWjKwyo

Tune 1.10 All Around the Maypole See How They Trot: https://youtu.be/qR_-IDEBPgA

Tune 1.11 Marybone Assembly: https://youtu.be/nDazw7-ywAc

Such a Wife as Willy Had with Ornaments: https://youtu.be/ShmpIt_pRuw

Tune 1.12 Fishes in the Sea: https://youtu.be/WpE3i03x87s

Tune 1.13 Favourite Banjo Breakdown: https://youtu.be/3Ylnnabj3oA

Tune 1.14 Sailors Hornpipe: https://youtu.be/ll8NZPvfpvY

Tune 1.15 The Cat's Polka: https://youtu.be/eiaTf0MA8DM

Tune 1.16 Beautiful Star https://youtu.be/dm2hrux7pmc

Chapter 2

Tune 2.1 Minasi Number 3: https://youtu.be/rXJkhbKCgF8

Tune 2.2 Minasi Number 7: https://youtu.be/CXRy9eormDE

Tune 2.3 Waltz: https://youtu.be/eKVe7XmEcBE

Tune 2.4 Tyroler Waltzer: https://youtu.be/X8NsiV8rrYs

Tune 2.5 Westwood Park: https://youtu.be/7mP_WxdIrnc

Tune 2.6 Litchfield Races: https://youtu.be/-uOQkLdLnFk

Tune 2.7 Lady Cathcart: https://youtu.be/1c6mSaLgYsU

Tune 2.8 The Exile: https://youtu.be/nIgwFWMza40

Tune 2.9 Birmingham March: https://youtu.be/oSp_ERG1OBM

Tune 2.10 The Labarynth: https://youtu.be/-Jt7BDVRogo

Tune 2.11 Tekeli: https://youtu.be/-uLpDafUjPA

Tune 2.12 Honey Moon: https://youtu.be/pYXcEr4PhmQ

Tune 2.13 Paddy Wack: https://youtu.be/w-sYAVr1Z8Q

Tune 2.14 Frogmore Farm: https://youtu.be/2RYkNMAnQVw

Tune 2.15 Miss Gayton's Hornpipe: https://youtu.be/CdVcCjLlIT8

Chapter 3

Tune 3.1 Ellingham Assembly: https://youtu.be/rfUmnffHQ24

Tune 3.2 Now or Never: https://youtu.be/JCB-RBgyNkI

Tune 3.3 King's Polka: https://youtu.be/fCH1cpf42JQ

Tune 3.4 The Philosopher's Jigg: https://youtu.be/mLPTzAF4hoA

Tune 3.5 Trip to London: https://youtu.be/O2wnr4g4Oo8

Tune 3.6 Saxon Hornpipe: https://youtu.be/kXNErHvDJdw

Tune 3.7 Take a Dance: https://youtu.be/Pi7AYhapJrk

Tune 3.8 The Unfortunate Cup of Tea: https://youtu.be/XXo5tu1kfwo

Tune 3.9 Wilkes's Wriggle: https://youtu.be/DjOMmE-t0Eo

Tune 3.10 The Fiddler's Jig: https://youtu.be/1NLWRXfITMI

Tune 3.11 Welsh Fusiliers: https://youtu.be/VlRidlxAU9Q

Tune 3.12 Cure of all Grief: https://youtu.be/7if32ntD8tw

Tune 3.13 Harliquin Air: https://youtu.be/mU8Tgeu6Ueo

Tune 3.14 Two and Two: https://youtu.be/GLg-pZ-0rZ4

Chapter 4

Tune 4.1 Union Waltz: https://youtu.be/CwkwM225kDY

Tune 4.2 The Buds of May: https://youtu.be/FtBaySSqaXY

Tune 4.3 Spring's Waltz: https://youtu.be/AmJ6yqHBeF8

Tune 4.4 Freedom and Liberty: https://youtu.be/xNnAlb2fThE

Tune 4.5 Rakish Highlandman: https://youtu.be/8blGRLZ3v3A

Chapter 5

Tune 5.1 Chamberlain Election: https://youtu.be/b0_URF-6QZk

Tune 5.2 Nineteenth of May: https://youtu.be/69PTuT2AbW4

Tune 5.3 The London Camp: https://youtu.be/d7uv4di63aQ

Tune 5.4 Marey's Dream: https://youtu.be/oeJ-uc2B_fs

Chapter 6

Tune 6.1a Cotillon: https://youtu.be/T6hWqHC-6-A

Tune 6.1b Cotillon: https://youtu.be/DYo5k6xpd8Q

Tune 6.2: French March: https://youtu.be/YYjrtuCVCeI

Tune 6.3 Prince William: https://youtu.be/pGbdbalfJiQ

Tune 6.4 When once I lay with another Man's Wife: https://youtu.be/KLMLRbIlrUw

Tune 6.5 Holborn March: https://youtu.be/Jpcobz8Q-34

Tune 6.6 Grano's March: https://youtu.be/GK0QIGqatxo

Tune 6.7 Windsor Terrace: https://youtu.be/u2ocB-Tr2no

Tune 6.8 Maid in the Woods: https://youtu.be/_2u1TIRK3y4

Chapter 7

Tune 7.1 Dover: https://youtu.be/Sev4cfI7xOI

Tune 7.2 Colchester: https://youtu.be/02S3q-CtpeU

Tune 7.3 Vespers Hymn: https://youtu.be/RLCFTBfqHTc

Tune 7.4 Bridgeford: https://youtu.be/iQmuZQyJ0TI

Tune 7.5 Cambridge New: https://youtu.be/Bw8PsG8vrkI

Tune 7.6 Cambridge Short Tune: https://youtu.be/l6PP5Meoof4

Tune 7.7 Oxford Tune: https://youtu.be/luUm37c1w1Y

Tune 7.8 The Martyrs Tune: https://youtu.be/1KtGFGV0Q2w

Chapter 8

Telemann 5th Fantasia for Flute: https://youtu.be/W64x8j4EbH4

Westhoff 4th Partita for Solo Violin: https://youtu.be/cHKjA3d6Kl0

BIO

Cohen Braithwaite-Kilcoyne is well known on the English folk scene for his work with the BBC Radio 2 Folk Award nominated trio 'Granny's Attic' and as a soloist. Originally from Birmingham in the English midlands, Cohen developed a love for concertinas and melodeons while still at primary school.

Cohen's main passion is for English traditional music and song, but his musical interests run broader than that, into Baroque music, ragtime and Victorian popular music- and he has been known to throw all of these into his performances and teaching.

Cohen is an experienced teacher and has worked with students of all ages in workshops in the UK and across Europe. In addition to this, Cohen is in high demand as a one-on-one tutor and working online and face-to-face, he has taught squeezebox playing to students across the world.

More information on Cohen's work can be found at www.cohenbk.com

Selected Discography

Below is a selected list of the albums that Cohen has appeared on from 2016 to the time of writing in 2021.

Solo and with Granny's Attic:

Granny's Attic, *Off the Land,* WGS416, 2016

Cohen Braithwaite-Kilcoyne, *Outway Songster,* WGS422, 2017

Granny's Attic, *Wheels of the World,* GRICD001, 2019

Cohen Braithwaite-Kilcoyne, *Rakes & Misfits,* GRICD003, 2021

Granny's Attic, *The Brickfields,* GRICD005, 2021

Other records featuring Cohen Braithwaite-Kilcoyne:

Mick Ryan, *Here at the Fair,* WGS428, 2019

Stick in the Wheel, *From Here: English Folk Field Recordings Volume 2,* SITW011, 2019

Becky Mills, *Tall Tales and Home Truths,* TECD414, 2019

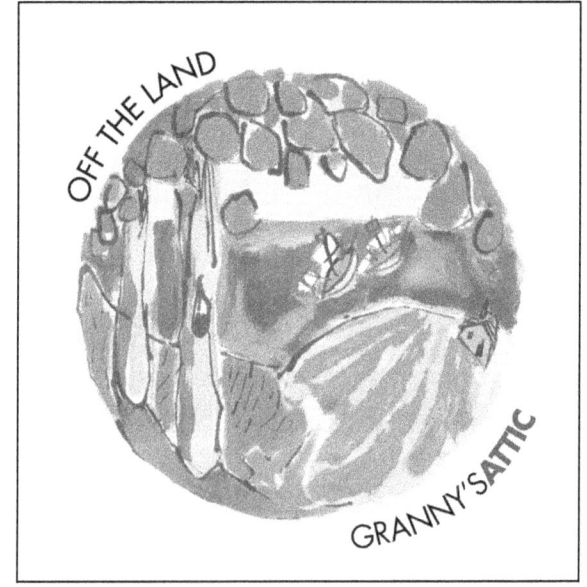
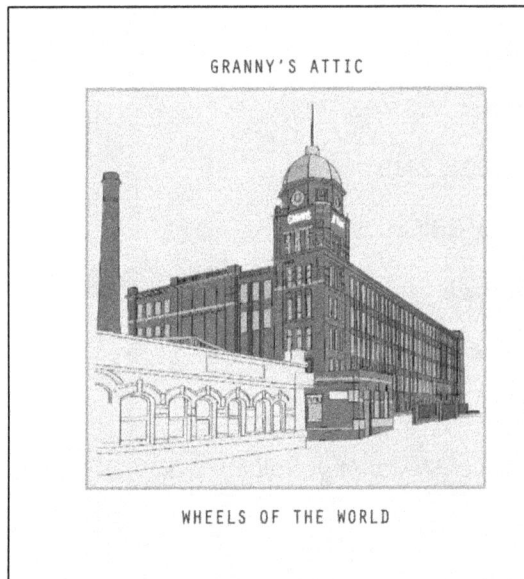

TUNE INDEX

All Around the Maypole See How They Trot 23

Beautiful Star 34

Birmingham March, The 49

Bridgeford 111

Bryan O'Lynn 14

Buds of May, The 84

Cambridge New 112

Cambridge Short Tune 113

Cat's Polka, The 33

Chamberlain Election 89

Christmas Tale, The 15

Colchester 109

Cotillon 96

Cotillon 97

Cure of all Grief 76

Devil in a Bush, The 18

Dover 108

Ellingham Assembly 58

Exile, The 47

Favourite Banjo Breakdown 31

Fiddler's Jig, The 73

Fishes in the Sea 30

Freedom and Liberty 86

French March 98

Frogmore Farm 54

Grano's March 104

Harliquin Air 77

Holborn March 102

Honey Moon 52

King's Polka 60

Lady Cathcart 46

Litchfield Races 45

London Camp, The	93
Magic Girdle, The	16
Maid in the Wood	106
Marey's Dream	94
Martyrs Tune, The	115
Marybone Assembly	25
Minasi Number 3	37
Minasi Waltz Number 7	40
Miss Gayton's Hornpipe	55
Nineteenth of May	91
Now or Never	59
Oxford Tune	114
Paddy Wack	53
Philosopher's Jigg, The	61
Prince William	100
Rakish Highlandman	87
Rattling Morgan	21
Sailor's Hornpipe	32
Saxon Hornpipe	64
Spring's Waltz	85
Such a Wife as Willy Had	14
Take a Dance	69
Tekeli	51
Telemann's 5th Fantasia – First Movement	118
Telemann's 5th Fantasia – Second Movement	120
Telemann's 5th Fantasia – Third Movement	123
Telemann's 5th Fantasia for solo flute	117
Tempest, The	22
Trip to London	62
Two and Two	78
Tyroler Waltzer	42
Unfortunate Cup of Tea, The	70
Union Waltz	83
Vesper's Hymn, The	110
Waltz	13

Waltz	41
Welsh Fusiliers	75
West Cottage Hornpipe	19
Westhoff's 4th Partita – Allemande	126
Westhoff's 4th Partita – Courante	128
Westhoff's 4th Partita – Gigue	132
Westhoff's 4th Partita – Sarabande	130
Westhoff's 4th Partita for solo violin	125
Westwood Park	44
When once I lay with another Man's Wife	101
Wilkes's Wriggle	71
Windsor Terrace	105

www.ingramcontent.com/pod-product-compliance
Lightning Source LLC
Chambersburg PA
CBHW081133170426
43197CB00017B/2849